CHASING FRANCIS

*Caution! Reading this book may cause spontaneous kindness, charity toward others, and a total overhaul of the way you think about what it means to be a follower of Christ.

> MARK BATTERSON, author of the *New York Times*
> bestseller *The Circle Maker*

In *Chasing Francis*, Ian Cron demonstrates that the deepest truths are best communicated with story. As someone who has experienced a bit of my own Italian pilgrimage with Francis, it is clear to me that these are not just words on a page, but the incarnated hope of a writer who has tasted something *real*.

> MICHAEL GUNGOR, recording artist, songwriter, and
> author of *The Crowd, the Critic, and the Muse: A Book for Creators*

If your heart longs for God, but you have questions — and have found aspects of your church experience to be less than the real thing — welcome to the club. But there's good news: centuries ago, the humble and joyful Saint Francis led the spiritually hungry away from "dead religion" and back to God himself — and through this wonderful book by my friend Ian Cron, he is doing it once again! Enjoy the ride.

> ERIC METAXAS, author of the *New York Times* bestsellers
> *Bonhoeffer: Pastor, Martyr, Prophet, Spy* and *Amazing Grace:*
> *William Wilberforce and the Heroic Campaign to End Slavery*

Ian Cron weds historical facts with his creative imagination to give us a twentieth-century feel for a saint who, more than anyone since New Testament days, lived out radical Christianity.

> TONY CAMPOLO, PhD, professor emeritus,
> Eastern University, and author

I've now read *Chasing Francis* twice and found it equally compelling both times. It's challenging, disarming, and delightful, and the vision behind it is a serious one. It's a remarkable book.

DR. ROWAN WILLIAMS, Archbishop of Canterbury

Chasing Francis is a wonderful story of pilgrimage and redemption, and Ian Cron's storytelling is so rich, bursting with details and insights, full of wisdom and warmth.

SHAUNA NIEQUIST, author of *Cold Tangerines* and *Bittersweet*

It's been said that God occasionally drops a handkerchief down to earth to leave God's scent in the world—and that those handkerchiefs are the saints. Ian Cron has picked up the handkerchief of this legendary figure, Francis of Assisi. There are tons of books about Francis that are historical and informative; in fact, it's been said more books have been written about Francis than any person in history other than Jesus. But this one's different, told through the life of a fictitious man named Chase. Dive in and allow God's fragrance to come off these pages and get on you. And then *be the fragrance* of God in the world like Francis was.

SHANE CLAIBORNE, author, activist, lover of Jesus

Francis of Assisi has never seemed more human and at the same time more God-drenched than he does here. *Chasing Francis* is absolutely seductive, not to mention also being the most adroit presentation of the saint that I have ever seen. This one is a feast for the soul as well as a great, churning, joyful romp for the spirit.

PHYLLIS TICKLE, author

It seems the world never gets tired of seeking, discovering, writing about, and falling in love with Francis of Assisi. Ian Cron does it again, but with real insight, imagination, and courage. Join in the chase!

FR. RICHARD ROHR, author of *Falling Upward: A Spirituality for the Two Halves of Life*

By guiding us to wrestle deeply with a crisis of faith experience and reintroducing us to a giant of faith, Ian Cron paves for us a path of grace, humility, and ultimate joy, even through our "ground zero" darkness. This is a life-changing work. I now find myself "chasing Francis" in my life as well as in my art.

MAKOTO FUJIMURA, artist and author

Ian Cron paints a beautiful, authentic, and vivid picture about people and God and gives all of us permission to tell our stories, complete with all of the shadows and fog and light. *Chasing Francis* encourages us to follow Jesus in both the joy and wreckage of life. You'll be changed, impacted, and transcended into a place where God can speak to you.

BRAD LOMENICK, president of Catalyst
and author of *The Catalyst Leader*

Before I read this compelling book, Francis of Assisi was someone I knew very little about. But now I realize he is someone who has always, somehow, known a great deal about me—about what my heart wants and about what it might look for me to chase ferociously after it.

JOSH JAMES RIEBOCK,
author of *Heroes and Monsters*

Funny, surprising, and profound, *Chasing Francis* invites readers on a pilgrimage—through history, through doubt, through the back roads of Italy, to unlikely holy ground. A masterful storyteller, Ian Cron delivers a tale that is both imaginative and relatable. It's the kind of book you are sorry to finish, the kind that sticks in your mind and heart long after the last page has been turned, as what begins as the story of someone else's journey turns out to be your own.

RACHEL HELD EVANS, author of *Evolving in Monkey Town* and *A Year of Biblical Womanhood*

✳

CHASING FRANCIS

A PILGRIM'S TALE

IAN MORGAN CRON

ZONDERVAN®

ZONDERVAN.com/
AUTHORTRACKER
follow your favorite authors

For Anne, Cailey, Madeleine, and Aidan—
Pax et bonum

✝ ✝ ✝

Resplendent as the dawn and as the morning star, or even as the rising sun, setting the world alight, cleansing it, and giving it fertility, Francis was seen to rise as a kind of new light.

Like the sun he shone by his words and works upon a world lying torpid amid wintry cold, darkness, and sterility, lighting it up with radiant sparks, illuminating it with the rays of truth, and setting it afire with charity, renewing and embellishing it with the abundant fruit of his merits, and enriching it wonderfully with various fruit-bearing trees in the three orders he founded. Thus did he bring the world to a kind of season of spring.

PROLOGUE TO THE
"LEGEND OF THE THREE COMPANIONS"

Life holds only one tragedy, ultimately:
not to have been a saint.
CHARLES PÉGUY

I

In the middle of the journey of our life
I came to my senses in a dark forest,
for I had lost the straight path.

Oh, how hard it is to tell
what a dense, wild, and tangled wood this was,
the thought of which renews my fear!
                        DANTE, *Inferno, Canto 1, lines 1–6*

AS ALITALIA FLIGHT 1675 BEGAN MAKING ITS FINAL DESCENT INTO
Florence, I nervously fanned the pages of my copy of *Divine Comedy*. Two decades of sitting in my damp basement had left a powdery coating of mildew that wafted into the air around me. For a moment I saw it, tiny specks and spores floating idly in the rays of sun pouring through the window. I hadn't read the *Inferno* portion of Dante's classic since I was an undergrad. At nineteen, of course, the freight those first few lines carried would have been utterly lost on me. Now, reading them with thirty-nine-year-old eyes, I wished I could call Dante up and schedule a lunch. I had a long list of questions for him.

Through the patina of condensation on the plane's window, I surveyed the Tuscan countryside below and knew I had lost the "straight path" and entered a "dense, wild, and tangled wood." Two weeks earlier, I'd been Chase Falson, founding pastor of the largest contemporary evangelical church in New England. My fourteen years in the ministry were a church growth success story. I'd considered myself one of the privileged few the heavens had endowed with a perfectly true compass. I'd known who I was and where I was going, and I'd been certain that one day I would see the boxes neatly checked off next to each of my life goals. I'd liked myself. A lot.

These days, lots of people dismiss you when they discover you're cut from evangelical cloth. Once you've been outed as a conservative Christian, they assume you're a right-wing, self-satisfied fundamentalist with all the mental acuity of a houseplant. Every Christmas, my Uncle Bob greets me at the front door of my parents' house, gripping a martini in one hand and a fat Cuban cigar in the other. He slaps me on the back and yells, "Look who's here! It's Mr. EEEeyah-vangelical!" It's disconcerting, but Bob's an idiot and suffers from an impulse control disorder.

For many a year, the terms *New England* and *evangelical* have been considered mutually exclusive. My church history professor told me that Jonathan Edwards referred to New England as "the graveyard of preachers." Baleful as that sounded, it didn't dissuade me from heeding the call to head east after seminary. My three closest friends were incredulous when I told them about my decision to start a church in Thackeray, Connecticut, a bedroom community thirty-five miles from Wall Street.

"Have you lost your mind? Even God's afraid of the Northeast," they said.

I laughed. "It's not so bad. I grew up there."

"But you could probably get a job at a megachurch somewhere," they argued.

Truth be told, I wasn't interested in working for a church someone else had built. I wanted to be the pioneer who "broke the code" for the spiritually barren Northeast, heroically advancing the cause of Christ into the most gospel-resistant region of the country. As a native, I was certain I knew the cultural landscape well enough to reach the Ivy Leaguers whose homes lay discreetly hidden behind stone walls and wrought-iron gates. A little self-important, but there you have it.

And yet, I had delivered the goods. I'd built a church where, at last count, over three thousand people came to worship every Sunday—a Herculean feat in a part of the world that's suspicious of things that are either big or new.

With the benefit of hindsight, I can see now that Putnam Hill Community Church had been built on the appeal of my belief in a God who could be managed and explained. I'd held such an unshakable confidence in my conservative evangelical theology that even some of the more skeptical locals had been won over. After I'd put in years of seventy-hour workweeks, Putnam Hill had become a church brimming with young Wall Streeters and their families, many of whom had come because they were disappointed that happiness hadn't come as optional equipment in their Lexus SUVs.

That world had detonated ten days ago. Gazing down on the terra-cotta roofs dotting the approaching Tuscan hills, I found myself on a forced leave of absence, and chances were good that when I returned home I would be out of a job.

✝ ✝ ✝

I have discovered that reaching the climax of a spiritual crisis in front of a thousand people is less than politic. In retrospect, I should have realized I was standing on the precipice of a yawning existential abyss. Subterranean streams of doubt had been leeching into the well of my most deeply held beliefs for two years. The scaffolding that supported my whole belief system was shaking as if some unseen force were trying to pull it down.

Three months before the cover came completely off the ball, I began meeting with Dr. Alistair McNally. "Mac" is a sixty-five-year-old psychiatrist, and the only decent therapist within a thirty-mile radius of Thackeray. Born and raised in Dublin, Mac had tousled shocks of white hair and a bawdy sense of humor. He's the only Christian shrink I know who doesn't make those annoying throaty humming sounds when you tell him some painful detail about your life. He doesn't insist on maintaining eye contact with you like a Martian practicing mind control, either. He's just a regular guy who has a lot more mileage on his odometer than I do, and I like him. Mac's secretary, Regina, is a member of our church, so we met outside the office under the guise of playing squash at his club. My erratic moods were fast becoming a topic of conversation at church. The last thing I needed was for people to find out I was seeing a psychiatrist.

One day, after he'd trounced me three games in a row, Mac and I sat on the floor outside the court, trying to catch our breath.

"So how are we doing this week?" Mac asked.

I heaved a sigh. "I actually feel worse than I did last week," I said. "I still can't sleep and I've gained three pounds. I've picked up a new hobby, though."

"What is it?" he asked.

"Road rage."

Mac laughed. "So what do you do when you can't sleep?"

"You mean when I'm not glued to the TV, eating gallons of ice cream?" I asked.

Mac chuckled again. "Yes."

"I spend a lot of time staring at the ceiling, questioning everything I've believed in for the past twenty years. I can't figure out what's come over me. I used to be 'Bible Man'—just push the button and I'll give you the answer. Next thing I know, I'm Bertrand Russell. Someone pulled the chair out from under my faith."

"And what 'faith' would that be?" he asked in his lilting Irish brogue.

"The uncomplicated one," I said. "Following Jesus used to be so tidy. Every question had a logical answer. Every mystery had a rational explanation. The day I walked across the stage to pick up my seminary degree, I thought I had God pretty well figured out. Everything I believed was boxed, filed, and housed on a shelf."

Mac wiped his brow with a towel. "Sounds like *Dragnet* theology," he suggested.

"What does that mean?"

"A 'just the facts, ma'am' kind of religion," he said.

"Yeah, but for twenty years that worked for me. Now I have more questions than answers."

"What kind of questions?"

"Dangerous ones," I replied with mock seriousness.

Mac smiled. "Give me a 'for instance,'" he said.

"For instance: Why do I have this sneaking suspicion that I've been reading from a theological script someone else wrote? Is this *my* faith, or one I bought into as a kid without really thinking about it? Why do I feel ashamed that I have doubts and questions? My faith used to be so full of life; now it all seems so beige. Sometimes I get so angry I want to punch a wall."

"How come?" Mac asked.

"I was sold a bill of goods," I said, tapping my racket head against the floor.

"By whom?"

"It's hard to put a finger on. The Christian subculture, I guess. That tiny slice of the world used to be all I needed. Now I think it overpromises and underdelivers."

For months, anything that even remotely smacked of evangelicalism had been posing a challenge to my gag reflex. I used to devour all those books that promised a more victorious spiritual life in three easy steps. I went to the pastors conferences where celebrity speakers with mouthfuls of white Chiclet teeth gave talks that sounded more like Tony Robbins than Jesus. I'd recently gotten a mailer advertising a seminar on church growth and evangelism at a megachurch. The theme of the convention was emblazoned on the header: "Take the Hill for Jesus!" It had a picture of the host pastor holding a Bible while standing next to an army tank.

I'd been shocked a few years before when a friend from seminary converted to Catholicism because he felt evangelicals had "McDonaldized" Jesus. I was starting to see his point.

"I don't think anger's the core issue here," Mac said. "The anger is masking another emotion."

"Which one?" I asked.

"Fear."

"Fear of what?"

"You're afraid that if you can't find a new way to follow Jesus, then you might not be able to stay in the game," he answered.

Mac stood up to get a drink from the watercooler. That a guy with skinny white legs, a generous paunch, and a concave butt could thrash me so badly at squash was a little embarrassing.

"How are things at the church?" he asked.

"I'm teaching a series in our young adult class called Absolute Truth in an Age of Relativism."

"How's that going?" he asked.

"Not so hot. I feel like I'm trying to answer questions no one's asking."

"Including you?" Mac asked gently.

I shrugged. "Maybe. What's discouraging is that our twenty- and thirty-somethings are leaving."

"Any idea why?"

"I pulled one aside the other day and asked her. She said I had 'way too many certainties' and our Sunday services were too slick. They're all heading off to some hip new church in Bridgewater where everyone seems to like candles and goatees."

Mac sat down on the floor to stretch his hamstrings. "Other pastors in town must be dealing with the same stuff. Have you talked to any?" he asked.

"I went to a clergy luncheon last week."

Mac rolled his eyes and chuckled. It was a notorious cast of characters.

"How'd it go?" he asked.

"It was a disaster. They had a speaker who railed about the culture wars and how we needed to pray that America would 'rediscover the faith of its founding fathers.'"

"Oh boy," Mac said.

"Afterward, the conservative pastors got in a huddle and talked about America's 'slide into the moral abyss' and how they needed to get their congregants to vote Republican. When I walked past the liberal table, I heard them talking about how they had to stop the 'crypto-fascist evangelicals' from taking over the country," I vented.

"What did you do?"

"I should've left, but I stopped at the conservative table for a few minutes," I said.

"And?"

"The conversation was so depressing I tried to bring a little humor to it. So I said, 'Maybe we should build bunkers and store up canned goods for the Apocalypse.'"

Mac's eyes got big. "How did that go over?" he asked.

"They scowled so hard at me I thought my hair would catch fire."

Mac's laughter echoed down the hallway.

"Seriously, Mac, I'm fed up with all the feuding between theological conservatives and liberals, the good guys and the bad guys. Everybody's so sure they've cornered the truth market. Every morning I want to throw open my window and yell, 'Tell me there's something more! There has to be something more!'"

We sat for a few minutes listening to balls ricocheting off the court walls. Every so often, we'd hear someone yell an obscenity over a mistake that had cost a point.

Mac stood up. "Did you ever see *The Truman Show?*" he asked.

"The Jim Carrey flick?"

"Go rent it. It'll give us something to talk about," he said.

I stood up slowly. I'd torn the ACL in my right knee when I was in boarding school, and today I'd forgotten to bring my brace. "OK," I said, intrigued by the assignment.

"I'm going home for three weeks to visit my mother. I'll call when I'm back, and we'll set up another appointment," he said. He held open the door to the court for me. "Care for another lesson?" he asked puckishly.

+ + +

On Saturday night, my student ministries' pastor Chip came over to eat pizza and watch *The Truman Show*. When it comes to youth ministry, Chip has everything a senior pastor wants and then some. He's good-looking, charismatic, athletic, plays the guitar, and parents think he walks on water. The only thing that annoys me about him is that he lives in a state of constant surprise. Anytime someone walks into a room, he stands up, yells "Dude!" and hugs them like he hasn't seen them in ten years. I should know; he does it to me about five times a day. I knew Chip was getting antsy. He's thirty-two, and he's been dropping hints that he doesn't want to work with kids much longer. I dread the idea of trying to replace him.

Mac was right. *The Truman Show* was great. Jim Carrey plays a guy named Truman Burbank who grows up in an idyllic town on a small island called Seahaven. What Truman doesn't know is that he's the star of the longest-running reality TV show in history. The island is a gigantic soundstage, his friends and family are actors, and five thousand hidden cameras beam his every move to the outside world. Gradually, Truman begins to realize something is amiss. He senses there's something beyond Seahaven, and despite everyone's attempts to keep him on the island, he becomes increasingly determined to leave and discover the truth.

One day he escapes in a small boat, sails through a violent storm, and crashes into the wall of the soundstage that's painted to look like the horizon. As he feels his way across it, he discovers a door and is faced with a decision. Does he return to his perfect life on the island, or does he walk through the door into whatever's waiting for him on the other side? In the final scene of the movie, Truman leaves the only world he's ever known and discovers the real world outside.

"Was that an amazing movie, or what?" I asked, turning off the TV.

Chip shrugged. "It was OK, I guess."

I stared at him. "What do you mean 'OK'? It was filled with layers of symbolism and meaning," I said.

"It wasn't as good as *Braveheart*. Besides, I like Jim Carrey's comedies better. *Dumb and Dumber* was freaking hilarious," he answered through a mouthful of pizza.

I stood up. "Are you serious? This movie's about the search for truth, for transcendence, for a higher reality. *Dumb and Dumber* isn't even in the same league," I replied.

"Have you seen it?" he asked.

I went red in the face. "No, but ..."

Chip stood up and began rummaging around in his pockets for his car keys. "It just didn't seem all that believable," he said. "Why would Truman want to leave the island?"

"You're kidding, right?" I asked.

"He had a pretty good life."

I was beginning to wonder if Chip and I had watched the same movie. In fact, I was beginning to wonder if we even lived in the same galaxy. "But, Chip—he couldn't possibly stay on the island. The whole thing was a lie!"

"Did you see how hot his wife was?" he asked.

"Chip, wake up!" I shouted.

Chip's face darkened, and he folded his arms across his chest.

"Chase, what's with you these days? I'm a little tired of being treated like an idiot. You asked me what I thought, and I told you," he said.

He was right. I'd been pushing his buttons a little hard lately. And I knew why. Chip was an icon of everything I'd begun to resent. He walked and talked the party line. He didn't question anything. He had a facile answer for every question the universe threw at him. I followed him to the front door with my tail between my legs.

"I'm sorry, Chip. I'm feeling a little burned-out these days," I said remorsefully.

"OK," he said, but I could tell it wasn't. "I better head home. I've got a big day tomorrow," he said yawning. "I told the senior highers they could shave my head if they raised enough money to underwrite our mission trip to Mexico. A bunch of them said they were going to bring their unchurched friends to watch," he said.

After Chip left, I went to bed and for the umpteenth night in a row had trouble falling to sleep. I played all the highlights of the film over and over in my head. It didn't take a genius to figure out why Mac had wanted me to watch the movie. I was Truman. I had begun to suspect there was something beyond the island of evangelicalism I'd been living on for twenty years. I was facing the very same kind of choice. Would I stay on that island, holding on to a relationship with God that increasingly felt vapid and unsatisfying, or would I leave and trust that there might be another way to follow him? Would I continue to lead our church down a path I was having trouble believing in anymore, or would I launch out and try to find another way? For a moment I felt a sense of hope and excitement—then came the "you're a very naughty dog" voice. The thought of leaving my little island terrified me. I started to feel desperate.

"Jesus, help me out here," I prayed. "Part of me wants to leave the island, and part of me can't imagine living life anywhere else."

Pulling the covers over my head, I slowly drifted off to sleep and passed the night dreaming about leaky boats and boiling oceans.

✢ ✢ ✢

The next morning at church I did something I'd never done before. Maybe watching *The Truman Show* had inspired me to step out and take a risk. I was preaching on the topic of worship when, toward the end of my message, I left my outline and began winging it. Sure, I'd gone off script for a sentence or two before, but this was full-blown excursus.

"I've been asking a lot of questions lately. What if God isn't as predictable and explainable as we'd like to think? I remember reading Faulkner's 'The Bear' for a freshman English class in college. In the story, a young boy named Ike McCaslin is tracking this elusive bear, a symbol for the all-powerful God. After a bunch of failed attempts, he figures out that if he wants to catch a glimpse of the bear, he'll have to leave behind his gun and compass and stand defenseless in the open. For a fleeting moment the glorious creature appears in the glade, glances over its shoulder at Ike, and melts back into the forest like a bass disappearing into the depths of a lake," I whispered.

As I spoke, I wondered why I hadn't done this before. I was vibrating on the inside, blood and adrenaline rushed through my veins. This was my "I Had a Dream" speech. I went on for several more minutes and then moved in for my closer.

"What if, now and then, we put the drums and guitars away, turned off the projectors, shut down the sound system, and waited quietly for God to emerge from the woods? Do we have enough faith to believe he'd appear to us as a community?"

I was enraptured. I'd spoken from a place in my soul that I always knew existed but didn't know how to access. What I said wasn't perfect, but it was perfectly me. I'm not sure what I had hoped would happen next. Maybe I'd envisioned a group of ecstatic congregants hoisting me onto their shoulders and parading me around the auditorium, chanting my name. Even a brief round of polite golf applause would have been nice. Instead, everyone looked as if huge doses of novocaine had been shot into their faces while I was speaking. I could hear the universe yawning.

After the service, several people told me that my sermon had been "interesting." That, I knew, meant I would get ten e-mails on Monday morning asking if I'd recently sustained a major head trauma. Before long, I started feeling a tad defensive.

The straw that broke the camel's back was Bill Archer. Bill's not one of our more relationally intuitive members. He's a loud, backslapping owner of a pest-control franchise whose ability to say the wrong thing at the wrong time is legendary. Whenever he opens his mouth you wonder where the bodies are going to drop.

"I've heard some sermons in my time, but that one takes the prize," he said, laughing wheezingly. Bill was in his early fifties, pudgy and pasty-skinned from too many years of chain smoking. "Where'd you get it, anyway? Off the Internet?" Bill gawked around at the group of newcomers I'd been talking with to see if any of them found his comments as funny as he did. They mostly looked embarrassed. Molten psychic lava began rising. It started at my ankles, passed through my knees and chest toward the top of my head. There was no way to cap the blast. I put my face so close to Bill's that I could have counted his nose hairs.

"Bill, why don't you sit down and give your mind a rest?" I said, through clenched teeth. The smile on Bill's face withered. He muttered something about my not having a sense of humor and slunk away. Things were going from bad to worse.

✛ ✛ ✛

It was a nine-year-old girl named Iris Harmon who broke me. I baptized Iris when she was three months old. Her mom, Maggie, was a thirty-five-year-old who had only recently gotten sober. Her AA sponsor, a member of our church, had told her that Putnam Hill might be a good place to put down roots and find a Higher Power. Maggie had grown up in the Catholic Church; even gone to Catholic schools—but her experience with Catholicism had left a bad taste in her mouth.

"When I did my Fourth Step in rehab, I had to deal with my resentments toward the nuns I'd had as teachers," she told me when we first met. "I'm pretty much past it. I can go and sit in the back of a Catholic church to pray now. I like how quiet they are."

Every Sunday at our post-service coffee hours, I hovered over this fragile ex-junkie who reeked of cigarettes and regret. She was chary as a rabbit, eyes darting in every direction, constantly checking for a quick escape route. One Sunday, I was walking her around our new fellowship center and stopped to introduce her to one of our elders. In the middle of conversation, Maggie casually dropped "the F-bomb." I thought my elder was going to cough up a Volkswagen. Later that year, Maggie and Iris found Jesus, and even though it took a little while to knead them into the dough, they eventually became family.

+ + +

I buried Iris four days before I blew up my life. She fell off her bicycle, hit her head on the curb, and never woke up. I was there when Maggie gave the doctors permission to turn off the respirator. After days of hearing machines and monitors buzzing and wheezing, the room became eerily silent. It was humid with despair. Maggie and I held hands and fixed our eyes on Iris's little form, a small-boned sparrow, hoping that the breath of God would revive her. But the *ruach* never came. Maggie ran her fingers over the outlines of Iris's knobby legs, limp and quiet beneath the white sheets, and whispered, "Oh, child," as though her girl had only bumped her head and run home to mama seeking solace.

It was a keening that could make the universe bow its head in sorrow and accord.

Maggie turned on me in the hospital parking lot. "So where's God now?" she said through gritted teeth. "I gave my life to Christ, did everything you told me. How could he do this?" Pools of rage gathered in Maggie's eyes.

Something pushed me beyond a border I hadn't known existed. From a room down deep in my soul I saw a hutch crammed full of antique china tip and begin to fall. I watched myself frantically running to stop it, but I couldn't get there in time. It exploded on the floor of my heart with a reverberating crash. Splintered wood and shards of china splashed through my soul as Maggie, trembling with anger, waited at the end of a long tunnel for me to answer. Standing over the wreckage, a voice dripping with contempt whispered, *Kiss everything good-bye.*

✝ ✝ ✝

I came to faith when I was a freshman at Stockford College in Danbridge, Massachusetts. There had been an unbroken line of Falsons at that wonderful old school for generations, going back to before the Civil War. I have a picture of me as a baby in my grandfather's arms wearing what looks like an unbearably coarse wool sweater with a large S on the front. From the moment of conception I was expected to be a Fighting Cardinal and a member of the DKE frat house one day.

I don't think there's a place more magical than Stockford in the fall. My first September there, I walked around the quad wondering if I'd been parachute-dropped into the classic seventies film *A Separate Peace.* The long line of ancient oaks and maples that shaded the sidewalk leading up to the entrance of Garnett Hall were ablaze with leaves so full of fire and glory that it produced a sweet melancholy in the center of my chest. The sheer beauty of that place made me yearn for something I couldn't describe but knew existed.

During freshman rush week, I met a really pretty girl named Leslie at a fraternity party. Late one night I walked her back to her dorm (with less than honorable intentions, I might add), and en route she told me she was a "Christian." No one had ever said that to me before, but it didn't matter; she was so pretty that she could've told me she was a toaster oven and I wouldn't have been put off.

"You really need to meet Phil Barclay," she said, with all the bubbling enthusiasm of a cheerleader.

"Who's he?" I couldn't have cared less, but I knew that keeping the conversation going was mission critical.

"He's the new InterVarsity staff guy on campus," she said.

"He works in the athletic department?"

Leslie laughed. "No, InterVarsity's a Christian organization. I know the two of you would hit it off. Come with me tomorrow night to our meeting and I'll introduce you," she said, batting her eyes. Little did I know that I'd been lured into the web of a brilliant evangelist.

+ + +

I wasn't a promising candidate for the whole "born again" thing. I had been raised in the cradle of Northeastern affluence, not the Deep South. I was the only child of urbane Episcopalians who didn't have even a passing interest in church. My mother was raised by strict conservative Baptists in a small rural town in eastern Colorado, a fact that was rarely discussed in our home. I had once heard her tell a friend that, after she arrived at Smith on an academic scholarship, she sloughed off the yoke of her "oppressively religious childhood" and embraced my father's more rarified spiritual roots. He claimed my mother's side of the family was "hectically enthusiastic" about religion and that the absence of alcohol at their wedding reception was still a source of embarrassment. I remembered coming home from boarding school and asking my father if our family were Christians.

"Good heavens, no," he said placing his hand over his heart and looking heavenward. "We're Episcopalians."

To say my parents' marriage was a disaster would be charitable. Life at home was like a scene from O'Neill's *Long Day's Journey into Night*. My father was a bumptious alcoholic who every night at five o'clock poured his first scotch. By seven-thirty he'd be walking around the house in a fog, bumping into doorframes and muttering apologies to no one in particular. Sometimes he'd stumble across me playing on the family-room floor and look confused, like he might try to introduce himself to me. My mother patrolled the house like June Cleaver, tidying up, lost in dreams about new upholstery. It takes a lot of psychic energy to maintain that kind of denial.

When Phil came along, I felt for the first time in my life that a man worth respecting was "seeing" me. I once read that a young man who doesn't have an older man who admires him is impoverished. If that's true, I was rich for the first time in my life. We spent long afternoons playing lacrosse on the grassy knoll in front of my fraternity or talking over dinner in the Lancaster Union. He listened to me as though every syllable of every word mattered. And yet there was a marked difference between Phil and me. He was solidly grounded, and I was an astronaut in zero gravity drifting through space. I could have written this off to his being ten years older than me, but I knew better. His feet were planted in another kingdom. Mine weren't planted at all.

Sitting in my dorm room late one night, Phil shared the gospel with me. It all seemed so logical and simple. The idea that I was the object of God's affection was intoxicating.

"Chase, can you think of any reason why you shouldn't pray to receive Christ right now?" Phil asked.

Holding back tears, I whispered, "I don't think so."

"All you have to do is surrender your heart to Jesus. Ask him to be the center of your life," he urged.

"How do I do that?"

Phil sat next to me on my bed. "You can pray with me to do it right now," he answered.

"You mean, out loud?" Beads of sweat formed on my brow and ran down my back.

"I can tell you how the prayer goes, and you can say it alone," he said reassuringly.

"What if I don't remember all the words?" I asked. At the time, I was taking a course called The Hebrew Scriptures as Literature. I'd read the first five books of the Old Testament and knew that hacking God off was a really bad idea.

"Don't worry, it's not about the words; it's about the heart," he answered.

I couldn't imagine praying out loud with someone else, especially a pro. "I think this is something I'd like to do alone," I said.

Standing on the steps of Jennings Hall, Phil shook my hand and said he'd call the next day to find out how I was doing. It was two in the morning when I walked out onto the quad, hands in my pockets and shoulders shivering. It was colder than normal for October. People living nearby had loaded up their woodstoves before going to bed, and the smell of burning oak sweetened the air. Gazing upward, I saw the aurora borealis for the first time. My grandfather had told me about it, but I still wasn't prepared for how beautiful it was—pillars of red and green light hanging like drapery in the heavens. I sat down on the steps of the college library, wading in a puddle of tears, and whispered yes to the night.

For the next four years, Phil and I met every Friday morning so he could "disciple" me. He led me to believe that if I just had a daily quiet time, went to church, tithed, shared my faith with others, and went to an accountability group, life would be manageable. He called the Bible "The Owner's Manual," and like most manuals, it was supposed to explain the way the machine worked. If you couldn't find the answer in the Word, you simply weren't looking hard enough. Phil was deep into apologetics. He loaded me down with books by authors who defended the rationality of faith and made me memorize the Four Spiritual Laws as though God had given them to Moses alongside the Ten Commandments. For a kid who grew up in complete spiritual chaos, this systematized brand of religion was appealing—so appealing that I bet my life on it.

I don't doubt that Phil meant well. Nor do I doubt that the Jesus who wooed and won my heart that autumn night is still real. It's just that somewhere along life's way I began yearning for something Phil never told me about.

✝ ✝ ✝

The next few days after Iris's memorial service were miserable days for me. I had nowhere to take my grief and confusion. I barely left my condo or answered the phone. At night I drank glass after glass of wine, hoping it would help me fall asleep, but it only made my head muzzy and my heart more leaden. One morning around three o'clock I called Mac, all lit up, and started leaving a weepy, incoherent message on his machine about how lonely I was. Suddenly I became incensed and told him I hated God and my church.

I was all over the road, weaving back and forth, bouncing off one guardrail and slamming into the other, sparks flying and hubcaps rolling. All the while I could hear the rumble of Sunday approaching like humming in the tracks before a freight train rounds a corner. I should have asked someone else to preach, but I wasn't the ask-for-help type. Big mistake.

That Sunday, the auditorium was jammed to the rafters. Every church has a child or two who belongs to everybody, and Iris was one of those kids. People hugged each other a little longer that morning, and there were still a few reddened eyes in the room. Folks had come out in droves that week simply because they needed to be together.

For three weeks I'd been giving a series of Lenten messages about the last words of Jesus. On that Sunday I was speaking on Jesus' mournful words, "I thirst." I'd prepared the talk over the summer: I was presenting my case for why thirsting for God wasn't necessary. My premise was that if we would just examine the biblical and historical evidence for the deity of Jesus, as well as the forensic case for the physical resurrection, we would inevitably come to the conclusion that the gospel was true. Simply believing these evidentiary facts, saying the Sinner's Prayer, and dedicating ourselves to a life of obedience would bring life-bearing water to our arid souls.

Everything was going fine until point three. It was then that the teeth of the cogs began to grind and break off. I heard the same terrible crashing sound I'd first heard in the hospital parking lot with Maggie. This time, however, the clamor was deafening. I looked down at my sermon text and understood for the first time what dyslexia must be like. It looked like all the words on my carefully scripted page had gotten into a multicar accident. I shook my head, hoping the letters would scurry across the clean white paper and reorganize themselves into cogent ideas. A knot balled up in my throat, and a wave of defeat and resentment washed over me. The gig was up. I desperately tried to recover and get back to my outline, but I was hurling toward earth. No amount of pulling back on the stick could get the plane out of its death spiral. For the second time in my life, I went off script.

"After I buried Iris this week, something happened to me," I said in a slow and tentative voice very different from my normal delivery. I wished I could speak in tongues, in some language of the Spirit that could convey to these people I loved what had happened to my soul. I gazed down—my heart was pounding so hard that the front of my shirt was pulsating. I wondered if people could hear it through my lapel mike.

"The night that Iris died, something died inside me too ... there was this voice in my head ... or rather, this hutch full of china crashing somewhere deep ... my faith didn't die suddenly ... it happened slowly ... I tried everything to get it back but...." I stopped and tried to regroup. Nervous coughs reverberated around the auditorium. Dizzy and nauseous, I sat down on the edge of the stage, knowing that nothing I was saying was making any sense to anyone, not even to me. I looked out at people whose weddings I had presided at, couples whose marriages I had helped mend, children I had baptized, men and women I had brought to faith. I was filled with a grief I had never known before and never wished to know again. And then, like an alcoholic at his first AA meeting, admitting out loud for the first time that he had a drinking problem, I confessed in an anguished voice, "My faith is gone."

Every ounce of oxygen was sucked out of the room. I looked up and saw Maggie sitting in the front row, nodding at me, a faint smile on her lips. It was as though she were encouraging a little boy in the first-grade school play to carry on even though he'd forgotten his lines.

I struggled on: "I used to have all the answers—just opened the Bible and there they were. The truth is, they *aren't* all there— or if they are, I can't find them. I've tried to convince you that Christianity is logical and straightforward, as if God can be codified and stuffed into files he can't jump out of. Every time uncertainty knocked on the door, I hid behind the couch until it went away. Now I'm the one who's thirsty." My throat was so tight it was painful, my voice strained and hoarse. "And the Jesus I've known for twenty years isn't making it go away."

I stood up. "And what about our church? I mean, is this all there is? People come in our doors hungry for God, we get them to sign a card that says they believe everything we do, and then we domesticate them." I opened my arms and looked toward the ceiling, "Putnam Hill—Everything You've Come to Expect in a Church and Less," I announced.

I was spent. The waters of my baptism ran down my face.

I shook my head. "Maybe we're all fools." And with that I shuffled down the center aisle and out the auditorium doors.

When I got to my office, I closed the door behind me and collapsed onto the leather couch I had placed beneath the large windows that looked over our grounds. A Thomas Kinkade print on the wall behind my desk was a gift from an elderly couple for officiating at their wedding. I stared at it quizzically. The warm idyllic light, the safety of a home in a forest—I felt like it was all laughing at me. I saw the world portrayed in that painting for what it was—nonexistent.

A few minutes later, the door to my office blew open and my senior elder Ed Dalton charged in. Ed's the retired CEO of one of the biggest airlines in the world. He liked to say that running an elder's meeting was nothing compared to negotiating with labor unions. He wasn't known for mincing words.

"What happened out there?" he asked.

"Ed, I—"

"Have you lost your mind?" he shouted.

I rubbed my eyes, hoping it would make him disappear.

"If you'd only give me a minute to—"

"I'm calling the elders together. When can we see you?"

"I'm not sure," I stammered. "I think I need a day to gather—"

"Not tomorrow, today."

I was too tired to fight. "Six o'clock?"

"Fine," he said, storming out as furiously as he had entered.

A few minutes later, I heard the sound of footsteps, followed by a gentle knock on the door. I was sure another member of the elder board had come to give me a piece of his mind, but there, God bless her, was Maggie—her eyes puddling with tears and pride. "That was the best sermon you've ever preached." In that moment of furious grace, Maggie folded me into her arms, and I wept.

✛ ✛ ✛

That night, six of our nine elders came to my condominium. I'd been bracing myself all afternoon for the moment when these men, all of whom I loved, would parade like a congress of crows down the geranium-lined slate path to my front door. Before they could ring the bell, I went to the screen door and silently held it open for them.

We sat in a circle in my living room. After a few minutes of waiting for someone to get the ball rolling, I gave my best shot at breaking the ice. Even I was taken aback at the edge of sarcasm in my voice. In just a few short hours, my remorse had morphed into anger and petulance. "I'd offer you guys something to drink, but coffee hour's probably over." The air in the room was so thick with anxiety that you could have cut it with a knife and served it as cake.

Ed spoke first. As senior elder it fell to him to be the designated hitter. "Chase, the elders met a few hours ago, and we've decided you need to take some time off." I'd never heard him speak in such an officious tone.

"How much time?" I asked.

"Enough for you to figure some things out, and—" He looked around at the men sitting in the room.

"And?" I asked.

Ed stared down at the rug and blew out a stream of air through his teeth. He looked older than I'd ever seen him before. "And enough time so the church can figure out what we need to do.

Even before what happened today, people were asking if you should move on from Putnam Hill. No one can deny the fact that you started this church. But you've changed."

Peter Collins spoke next. Peter, Thackeray's most beloved pediatrician, was a fine soul. For years, he'd called me every week just to ask how I was doing personally. "You haven't been yourself for a while, Chase," he said.

"We know about your meetings with Dr. McNally, too," interrupted Hal Frick, sounding like the Wicked Witch of the West. Apparently, Mac's secretary, Regina, had the gift of gab. "Your moods are spooking the staff—and God knows you owe Bill Archer an apology," he added. Bill and Hal were best friends. They deserved each other.

I slumped down in my old wingback chair. "So what are you proposing?" My anger was becoming shame. It was a pattern I'd perfected.

Ed continued. "We want you to take a leave of absence. Chip can handle things around here while you're gone."

I was dumbstruck. Fourteen years of backbreaking work left in the hands of a guy who liked *Dumb and Dumber*.

"And then what?" I asked.

"Let's not get ahead of ourselves. We'll meet with you when you get back and see where we are," Ed answered.

Sweet old Marvin Ballard. He never spoke much at meetings, but wherever he went he brought a godly presence. "I'm sorry, Chase," he muttered.

I don't remember much of what was said after that or what the others thought. There was a discussion about my continuing to be paid, and how I shouldn't come into the office or communicate with members of the church. I assume they were afraid I might launch a campaign to keep my job and end up splitting the church. When all was said and done, I walked them to the door. Just when I thought the worst of the storm had passed, Ed turned to me and said, "Chase, you and I started this church together. Perhaps I never told you, but I've always loved you like you were one of my own sons. What you did today broke my heart. Maybe I should have seen you were going off the rails, but I never imagined you were capable of doing what you did today. I've never been as disappointed in a man as I am in you right now."

For the first time in our fourteen-year friendship, I saw tears pool in the corners of Ed's eyes. Every last stronghold of defiance on my part fell away. I longed to be held by that man while I begged his forgiveness. There was a wrecking ball swinging out of control in my heart.

"I sure hope you can pull yourself together," he finished. Not waiting for me to answer, he walked away. It was just as well. I had nothing to say.

II

The geographical pilgrimage is the symbolic
acting out of an inner journey.
THOMAS MERTON, *Mystics and Zen Masters*

Francis wished that everything might
sing of pilgrimage and exile.
THOMAS OF CELANO, *St. Francis of Assisi*

FOR THREE DAYS AFTER MY MEETING WITH THE CHURCH LEADER-
ship, I didn't set foot out of my condo. I was terrified of seeing
someone from the church in a store or on the street. I had Chinese
food delivered, drank toxic amounts of Diet Coke, and watched
reruns of *Everybody Loves Raymond*. I tried to get hold of Mac, but
his voice mail said he was still out of town and wouldn't be checking his messages until he returned. That's when I got the idea to
call Uncle Kenny.

Kenny is my mother's first cousin, but because they were so
close as kids growing up, my mother insisted I call him Uncle.
After college, Kenny turned down law school to teach high school
English in Durango, Colorado. When he was thirty-nine, his
pregnant wife, Susan, was returning home from visiting her family in Wisconsin when the commuter jet she was on overshot the
runway at the airport in Colorado Springs. Everyone on board
was killed instantly. The family said he never fully rebounded
from the loss. The proof lay in the fact that two years later, he did
the unthinkable—he left the conservative Baptist fold and became
a Catholic. Not only did he become a Catholic; he went on to

become a Franciscan priest. A conservative Baptist becoming a Catholic is like the pope becoming a Mormon. The long-haul viability of the cosmos is drawn into question when stuff like this happens.

Maybe it was because my mom had already left the conservative Baptists to become an Episcopalian that she didn't share the rest of the family's horror at Kenny's conversion. He had joined her as a fellow member in good standing of the Black Sheep Club.

Until I was about nine, Kenny came to our home for all the big holidays. I looked forward to his visits every bit as much as I looked forward to the arrival of Santa Claus and the Easter Bunny. His face was leathered from years of being outdoors in the Colorado sun, and his eyes were a startling cobalt blue. He'd chase me around the yard and take me fishing for smallmouth bass at the reservoir down the hill from our house. He was one of those souls who seemed at home with God. Though just a boy, I knew there was something luminous about him. Unlike my father, Kenny was consummately aware of the people around him. Despite his tenderness, he was demanding. He wouldn't tolerate your being anything less than your best — but there was a safety net of grace in his heart in the event you couldn't deliver.

Kenny's mind was every bit as supple as his heart was kind. After becoming a priest, he continued his studies at the Gregorian University in Rome and became a respected spiritual director. After twenty years of tending to the souls of would-be priests, he had gone into semiretirement. Now he divided his time between friaries in Assisi and Rome.

I'm not sure what inspired me to call him. It had been years since the two of us had spoken at length. When I called, a young postulant at the friary told me in halting English that Kenny was saying Mass. Two hours later, the phone rang and I heard that familiar voice, filled with all the grace and compassion I remembered as a child. I didn't know how to find my way into the reason

I'd called. For a few minutes we spoke about family until Kenny zeroed in. "Chase, you didn't call me to catch up, did you?"

"Uncle Kenny, I'm in trouble," I said.

There was a brief silence on the other end. "What kind of trouble?" he asked calmly.

I breathed out a sigh. "God trouble."

"Ah," he said.

Obviously, this kind of confession wasn't unfamiliar to a spiritual director. In two hours I told him everything. I recounted my meltdown in the service. I told him about my disillusionment with the church, and about my floundering faith. "I can't go on like this, Kenny. I'm sure there's another Jesus I haven't met yet. How on earth do I find him?"

I stopped to take a breath, and Kenny took advantage of the pause. "Come to Italy," he said.

"What?"

"Come to Italy."

I was about to say I couldn't possibly come to Italy when it dawned on me that of course I could. The elders had asked me to take a hike, and I couldn't stay locked in my condo forever. "Are you sure? I don't want to put you out," I said.

"It would be fun. Besides, I know someone who can help you," he said.

"It's not an exorcist, is it?" I said. "I know you Catholics are way into exorcists."

"No," he laughed. "He's not an exorcist."

"What should I bring?" I asked.

"An open heart, an open mind. Oh, and bring a journal."

"A journal? Why?"

"Trust me," he said.

It wouldn't be the last time I would hear those words. Five days later, I left for Italy.

✝ ✝ ✝

Walking through the Florence airport, I felt the same anxiety unaccompanied children must feel after a long flight. I'd always felt sorry for those poor kids. An overly cheerful airline employee with a walkie-talkie usually meets them at the gate, sticks an over-sized smiley face on their chests, and escorts them to their hand-wringing relatives waiting in baggage claim. As I walked off the plane, I longed for a comforting escort to help me find Kenny. I'd even have endured the smiley face on my chest.

Luckily, the airport in Florence is small. It wasn't hard to figure out that the man standing next to the baggage carousel wearing the hooded brown habit with the simple corded rope tied around his waist was probably Uncle Kenny. In the bedlam of the airport, Italians yelling and waving their hands at each other (Italians wave their hands and yell in their sleep), Kenny stood serenely as though he were the hub of a mysterious prayer wheel around which the world was compelled to revolve. Apart from his attire, he looked like an aged version of the cowboy who used to appear in the old Marlboro ads. Six foot two and wiry, his face played host to a concatenation of deeply furrowed lines. I smiled when I saw him smoking a cigarette, wearing Birkenstocks, and carrying an ancient leather backpack over his shoulder.

"Hello, Uncle Kenny," I said.

He turned around. His eyes widened, filled with strength and gentleness. He enveloped me in his tunic and whispered into my ear, "Hello, Chase Falson. Hello."

✝ ✝ ✝

When God created language, he neglected to include words that could do justice to the dazzling beauty of the old city of Florence. The burnished cobblestones that pave the streets tell stories of days long since forgotten. Kenny dropped me off at my hotel, then left to run some errands. He promised to be back in time to pick me up for what would be the most memorable culinary experience of my life. "Trust me," he shouted through the passenger window, "you've never eaten until you've dined in Firenze."

Kenny's car began to pull away from the curb. "When do I meet the exorcist?" I yelled.

"Tonight!" he cried as he sped away.

I'm not sure why Kenny booked me into the Helvetia & Bristol, one of the most expensive and lavish hotels in Florence. Built at the end of the nineteenth century, each room conjures up memories of Florence's glorious history. When the bellman opened the door to my room, it took my breath away. There were thick silk curtains, spectacular pieces of art, elegant appointments, and views of the Duomo.

After I unpacked my bags and got settled, I went downstairs and stood outside to wait for Kenny. On the adjacent corner sat an abandoned carousel, its lights long extinguished and its song quieted. The painted wooden horses were caught in suspended animation, bearing no happy riders. Staring at it, I wondered who Kenny was bringing to dinner. My "exorcist." Was he another priest, a therapist?

My thoughts about the mysterious stranger were quickly put on hold when I caught sight of Kenny's old Fiat shooting across traffic. A group of bike riders yelled and made hand gestures I'd never seen back home, though it wasn't hard to guess what they meant. The car screeched to a halt at the curb directly in front of me. It was like something Mel Gibson would have driven in *The Road Warrior*.

Between the condition of the car and Kenny's ability as a driver, getting to the restaurant was an exercise in the building up of my faith.

Kenny wasn't exaggerating about the food. The meal was a foretaste of the great eschatological banquet—salad, warm bread, linguini in a pink vodka cream sauce tossed with smoked salmon and peas, served alongside copious amounts of red table wine. When the last course was cleared away, I knew that everything I had ever eaten before that night was but a shadow of what God intended food to be.

"I'd hoped your friend would join us for dinner. Is he coming for dessert?" I asked.

"No, I don't think so," Kenny said.

I was a little crestfallen. "So when do I get to meet him?" I asked.

Kenny poured a little more wine into each of our glasses. "The identity of my friend may come as a bit of a surprise."

"Who is he?" I asked.

"His name is Giovanni di Pietro di Bernardone."

"Is he a Franciscan?"

"He's definitely a Franciscan."

"So who is he?" I asked impatiently.

"Saint Francis of Assisi."

I dropped my spoon. I may be an evangelical Protestant, but I know that Francis is a Catholic saint from the thirteenth century who's famous for holding up concrete birdbaths in people's backyards.

"You're kidding, right?"

Kenny took a sip of wine. "No, Francis is —"

"You think a guy who's been dead for eight hundred years can help me?"

"I know it sounds crazy, but —" Kenny said.

I looked at him out of the corner of my eye. "Kenny, you're not suggesting I become a Catholic, are you?" I didn't think my grandmother's Baptist ticker could survive another member of the family becoming a "papist."

Kenny laughed. "Don't worry, I'm not out to convert you," he said, lighting a cigarette.

I was so knocked off kilter that I didn't know how to respond. I was trying to wrap my mind around the fact that I had traveled all the way to Europe to meet a dead guy. I leaned forward. "Kenny, why didn't you tell me this on the phone?"

"Would you have come if I had?" he asked. I was silent. "Chase, give me thirty minutes to make my case. If I can't convince you to stay, I'll buy you a first-class ticket home. Deal?"

What could I say? I felt like I was standing there with a yellow smiley sticker on my chest. "OK," I said.

Kenny pulled his chair around the table to get closer to me. "After we spoke the other night, I realized that a priest in the Middle Ages could have come to one of his superiors and shared the same kind of disillusionment," he said.

"I find that hard to believe."

"Don't be so sure. The Middle Ages were an age of transition, and people were fed up with the old way of following Jesus."

"And that's where Francis comes in?"

Kenny nodded. "Just when the reputation of the church and Christendom was at an all-time low, Francis came along."

"What do you mean by Christendom?" I wanted to be sure we were talking about the same thing.

"Sometimes we use that term to refer to the part of the world inhabited by Christians. But really, there is a narrower sense in which Christendom was an ideal that was an inspiration over the centuries," Kenny explained. "Francis gave it life again and saved it."

I raised my eyebrows. "*Saved* it? How?"

Kenny waved to the waiter to bring us coffee. "By being a complete fool," he said.

"Come again?"

"Francis was crazy enough to live more like Jesus than anyone else in history, and it changed the world. People still call him 'the last Christian,' " he said.

I folded my arms across my chest. "And you think he can do the same thing today? Save the church?" I asked.

"It could use his advice," he said. "How much time do I have left to make my pitch?"

I smiled and looked at my watch. "Another twenty-six minutes."

Kenny blew out a stream of blue smoke. "How am I doing?"

"You still haven't made the connection between me and Francis."

"Here's what I'm thinking. Let's do some traveling. Let's visit places where important things happened in Francis's life and see what happens," he said.

I leaned across the table. "That's it?" I asked.

"Yeah," Kenny said.

"I'm having a nervous breakdown, and you want to take me on a guided tour of Franciscan shrines?"

"I don't lead tours," Kenny said indignantly. "We're going on a pilgrimage."

"A pilgrimage?" I imagined the two of us crawling up ancient marble stairs on bloodied knees to touch a weeping statue of the Virgin Mary. I'd seen this stuff on the Discovery Channel before, and it always gave me the willies. "Kenny, I'm a Protestant. We don't do pilgrimages."

Kenny snubbed out his cigarette in the ashtray. "You don't know what a real pilgrimage is, do you?" I thought about winging an answer but kept silent.

"The word *pilgrimage* comes from the Latin word *peregrinus*, which means a person wandering the earth in exile, someone in search of a spiritual homeland. If I'm not mistaken, that sounds a lot like you."

It was hard to argue with him on that score.

"Think of it this way," he continued. "A pilgrimage is a way of praying with your feet. You go on a pilgrimage because you know there's something missing inside your soul, and the only way you can find it is to go to sacred places, places where God made himself known to others. In sacred places, something gets done to you that you've been unable to do for yourself."

I signaled the waiter for more coffee. I knew I would regret it later, but the jet lag was beginning to catch up with me. "Kenny, I don't want to sound rude, but what you're describing sounds a little spooky."

"Have you ever heard anyone talk about 'the spirituality of place'?"

"No."

"When a pilgrim visits a sacred place and hears the story of what happened there, something mystical happens. The spiritual energy from that past event is released and speaks to the heart of the pilgrim. Especially when you combine it with a ritual."

"You believe that?" I asked.

"It sounds far-out, but it's actually not uncommon. Do you remember the time I took you to Yankee Stadium?"

"Of course I do." It was one of my most cherished childhood memories. My father refused to take me to baseball games because he thought it was the sport of the hoi polloi. I was indebted to Kenny for passing on his love of the game to me.

"Do you remember how you felt when we walked into the park? How awestruck you were when you saw the field and heard the roar of the crowd? I bet you remembered the story of a famous player who hit a game-winning home run to clinch a series and you said, 'That happened here.' Then we went through the ritual of putting on our Yankee caps, buying hot dogs, waving pennants, and singing 'Take Me Out to the Ball Game' with everybody else. And what happened? Ritual met space, and the energy of every glorious moment in that stadium was released. We felt something transcendent. That's what I'm talking about," he said.

I shook my head. "Kenny, I appreciate everything you want

43

to do for me, I really do. I'm just not sure this kind of thing is for me."

"Christians have been going on pilgrimages since the time of Jesus."

"Kenny—"

"Ever heard of Thomas Merton?"

Now he had my interest. Merton was a Trappist monk whose books about the contemplative life had made him famous in the fifties and sixties. As a young Christian, I'd gone through a serious Merton phase. "Sure, I've read some Merton," I said. Actually, I'd read everything he'd ever written.

"Merton was a strong believer in pilgrimages and the spirituality of place. He was drawn to sacred sites, not because he knew the places, but because he believed the places knew him."

"Kenny, don't you think this is slightly irrational?" I asked.

"Who said God's always rational?"

Three years before, that question would have sparked a heated intellectual debate. I'd have put C. S. Lewis or Lee Strobel on the witness stand and eaten Kenny for lunch. Given all that had happened, however, I'd softened to the idea that God might have an illogical side.

Kenny cocked his head. "Are you in?"

I peered into Kenny's eyes and wondered if I could trust him. How did I know he hadn't lost his mind since I last saw him? "I'm not sure this is what the doctor ordered. But—the patient is desperate. I'm in."

Kenny placed his hand on top of mine. "Don't worry. God will show up."

I smiled. "So we're going on a road trip?" I asked.

"Yep."

Kenny grabbed his backpack from under the table and began handing me books and packets of articles.

"What's all this?" I asked.

"Homework," he answered. I looked at some of the titles—
St. Francis of Assisi by G. K. Chesterton; *The Road to Assisi: The
Essential Biography of St. Francis* by Paul Sabatier; *Francis of Assisi: A
Revolutionary Life* by Adrian House; *Francis: A Call to Conversion* by
Duane W.II. Arnold and C. George Fry; *Reluctant Saint: The Life
of Francis of Assisi* by Donald Spoto; *St Francis of Assisi: A Biography*
by Johannes Jørgensen.

I stacked the books on the table. "Will there be a test?" I asked.

"Count on it."

I had been right about the coffee. When Kenny dropped me
off at the hotel, I was completely wired. Too many doubts and
hopes swirled in my head. I'd been elevated from low-church
Protestant to Catholic mystic in a mere thirty-six hours. *That's got
to be some kind of record*, I thought. I pulled out one of the articles
Kenny had given me: "St. Francis: Postmodern Saint." It was just
twenty pages, so I read it twice. I grabbed my journal, sat on the
edge of my hotel windowsill overlooking the Palazzo Strozzi, and
began taking notes.

Journal Entry:
The Helvetia & Bristol

*Just finished reading this article about Saint Francis. The introduction
takes a quote from The Francis Book. "Rembrandt painted him,
Zeffirelli filmed him, Chesterton eulogized him, Lenin died with his
name on his lips, Toynbee compared him to Jesus and Buddha, Kerouac
picked him as patron of the 'Beat' generation, Sir Kenneth Clark called
him Europe's greatest religious genius." That's quite a list of admirers.*

*Francis was born in the Middle Ages (c. 1181) in Assisi, a small
town in Umbria. The era Francis lived in and the one we live in today
are very different, but the article points out a few interesting parallels.*

*First, Francis lived in the gap between two historical periods—the
Middle Ages and the pre-Renaissance (the opening days of modernity).
We're living in the synapse between two moments in history as well—*

modernity and postmodernity. People in Francis's time felt the same anxiety that comes from living in a rapidly changing society that we do today. Another similarity between the Middle Ages and today has to do with the state of Christendom. In Francis's day, the church was hemorrhaging credibility. It was seen as hypocritical, untrustworthy, and irrelevant. Some people even wondered if it would survive. Clergy were at the center of all kinds of sexual scandals. It had commercialized Jesus—selling pardons, ecclesiastical offices, and relics. Sermons were either so academic that people couldn't understand them or they were canned. Popular songs ridiculing the church and clergy could be heard all over Europe. The laity felt used by the professional clergy, as if they were there to serve the institution, not the other way around. The church had also become dangerously entangled in the world of power politics and war. Some fringe groups were beginning to say you couldn't be a Catholic and a Christian at the same time. Disillusionment with the church inspired many people to turn to astrologers and other alternative spiritualities.

The demise of feudalism and the return of a money economy brought the rise of the merchant class and a ferocious spirit of aggressive capitalism. Greed ran riot in the culture. To top it all off, Christians were at war with Muslims.

OK, it all sounds eerily familiar.

The article's author believes Francis is a prophetic model for Christians in postmodernity. In the middle of huge cultural shifts, when the church was on the verge of collapse, Francis inspired thirty thousand people to model their lives after his—and they saved Christendom. Eight hundred years later, people are still trying to imitate him.

The writer says that postmoderns are good at criticizing the old way of doing things but not very good at offering alternatives for going forward. Francis didn't criticize the institutional church, nor did he settle for doing church the way it had always been done. He rose above those two alternatives and decided that the best way to overhaul something was to keep your mouth shut and simply do it better. It's like Gandhi said: "Seek to be the change you wish to see in the world."

The article was quick to point out that we shouldn't idealize Francis. Like all revolutionaries, he had his dark side. It also said we shouldn't look at the medieval period through rose-tinted glasses. What we should do, he says, is revisit some of our premodern sources to help us map the future of ministry in postmodernity. Interesting idea.

Is it possible that Francis intuited what the darker side of modernity would end up being long before it flowered? Was he postmodern in spirit before modernity even got off the ground? I think my learning curve over the next few weeks is going to be steep.

I'm finally feeling tired, but I just remembered something. When I was an undergrad, I had to read this play by an Italian named Luigi Pirandello titled Six Characters in Search of an Author. The plot deals with these six characters from an unfinished play that unexpectedly show up at a real play rehearsal in search of an author who can finish their story. Oddly enough, that's how I feel tonight. It's not like I've become an agnostic or an atheist. It just feels like I don't know my Author anymore. In a sense, I really am like Truman. I want to see what's behind the door. I want to find a new church and a new way to follow Jesus. If going on a pilgrimage with Kenny can help, then so be it. I'm also thinking of the last thing Kenny said to me before he pulled away from the hotel. "Chase, do you know what I'm looking forward to most of all? Just getting time with you." I almost lost it. It's been a long time since I had a friend. That may sound self-pitying, but that's where I live right now.

God, I really am a pilgrim in search of a new spiritual home. I've been evicted from my old one. See you in the morning.

III

The real voyage of discovery consists not in
seeking new landscapes, but in having new eyes.
MARCEL PROUST

I WOKE EARLY THE NEXT MORNING AT FIVE TO THE SOUND OF
garbage men collecting the trash. If the joy that people find in
their work is measured by the amount of noise they generate while
doing it, then these guys were in the throes of ecstasy. They sang,
they yelled, they whistled, they banged trash cans together. I
expected to look out the window and see a fully staged version of
Verdi's *Rigoletto*.

Abandoning any hope of going back to sleep, I made my way
to the bathroom to get ready for the day. European bathrooms
are where unsuspecting travelers generally discover the breadth
of their idiocy. I turned on the shower, not realizing it was one
of those arrangements where the showerhead isn't permanently
attached to the wall. Without warning, the shower hose took off
like a rocket and thrashed around the bathroom like an angry
cobra, violently spitting venom in every direction while I flailed
around the floor of the bathtub in my boxers attempting to wrestle the plumbing into submission. Even Mother Teresa would have
laughed at me.

Driving home from dinner the night before, Kenny had given
me the itinerary for the next day. "I'm going to pick you up at ten
o'clock. Our first stop is at a church here in Florence, and then
we're off to San Damiano," he said.

"Where's that?" I asked.

"Below Assisi," he replied.

I had four hours before Kenny arrived, so I dropped off my bags at the front desk, threw my book-laden backpack over my shoulder, and went out into the empty streets in search of espresso and a place to read and write. Even though he hadn't opened shop yet, a waiter at a café on the Piazza della Repubblica took pity on me and made me a double espresso. I closed my eyes and breathed in the earthy aroma of the dark brew before I drank it. I took out my journal and began to write.

Journal Entry:
The Café Concerto

Francis was a nutcase, but there's something so genuine about him that it's hard not to like him. He wanted to become a knight and fight in the regional wars that often broke out between Assisi and the neighboring towns. Francis was long on fashion — his father outfitted him in the latest knightly apparel — but unfortunately he was short on skill. In a war with Perugia, Francis was taken prisoner and spent a year in prison waiting for Dad to pay a ransom for his release. After he returned home, Francis was ill but refused to give up his dream of seeking glory as a knight — he signed up to go into battle again. So much for the "fool me once" rule. The night before the battle, Francis had a dream that changed his life. He heard a voice ask, "Who can do more good for you? The lord or the servant?" Perplexed, Francis replied, "The lord." The voice in his dream responded, "Then why are you abandoning the lord for the servant?" In a flash, Francis figured out who was speaking and said, "O Lord, what do you want me to do?" And the voice said, "Return to Assisi, and what you are to do next will be revealed to you."

So Francis turned around and headed back to Assisi. (A little shamefaced, I'm sure. There are probably few things more embarrassing than shooting off your mouth about how you're riding out to kick some butt, only to slink back into town a few days later claiming that God told you to go home.)

Soon after returning, Francis went to a little church dedicated to St. Damian to pray for guidance. The chapel at San Damiano was in shambles. The roof had caved in, the walls were cracked, and the altar was covered in debris. There were scant reminders that this had once been a thriving place of worship. The two most obvious were the words DOMUS MEA, "My House," written over the doorway leading into a side chapel, and a Byzantine crucifix hung over the chancel from which Jesus looked down over the ruins of the building. Historians say the dilapidated San Damiano was a metaphor for the disrepair of the church at large.

If Francis came to San Damiano to hear from God, he didn't leave disappointed. Bonaventure writes, "There as he knelt in prayer before a painted image of the Crucified, he felt greatly comforted in spirit and his eyes were full of tears as he gazed at the cross. Then, all of a sudden, he heard a voice come from the cross and telling him three times, 'Francis, go and repair my house. You see it is falling down.' Francis was alone in the church and he was terrified at the sound of the voice, but the power of its message penetrated his heart."

Looking up from my journal, I stared out at a group of old men feeding pigeons and thought about the condition of God's house in the twenty-first century. As far as I could tell, it was the only thing in the universe that duct tape couldn't fix.

Lost in thought, I didn't see Kenny sneak up on me. It's just as well. A conniving Franciscan is enough to make a person think.

"Tough day to be an atheist, isn't it?" he boomed. I spilled espresso up and down the front of my shirt. He found the whole scene very amusing.

"Yes, apart from being bushwhacked by a friar, it's perfect out," I said, scrambling to find a napkin.

"Where are your bags?" Kenny asked.

"With the concierge," I replied.

"Some of my novices are going to Assisi later, so I'll have them pick them up," he said. "Ready to go?"

I gathered the stack of books into my backpack. "I think so."

"*Andiamo!*" he said, and a flock of frightened pigeons flew into the cloudless Italian sky.

✢ ✢ ✢

The Brancacci Chapel is located inside the church of Santa Maria del Carmine on the other side of the Arno River. To get there, you have to cross the Ponte Vecchio, a fabulous stone bridge built in 1345. Every morning, merchants whose shops and stalls line either side of the bridge get ready for the swarm of tourists who will come to buy their expensive jewelry, while restaurateurs are busy hosing down the sidewalks and firing up their ovens for the midday meal. Kenny picked me up on a bright red Vespa scooter he'd borrowed from a friend, and he drove it like one of his sacred vows was never to use the brakes. At first I couldn't figure out why all the nice people on the bridge looked so surprised to see us. That was before I saw the sign saying that vehicles weren't allowed on the bridge. Kenny steered us through a sea of expletives, waving and smiling at the fuming tourists and vendors in his wake—to him, everyone was a friend.

Churches in Florence are like Starbucks in Manhattan—they're everywhere. Sadly, it doesn't take long to become callous to their number, as well as to their towering splendor. When we pulled up to the church of the Santa Maria del Carmine, however, I sensed there was something extraordinary about it. Walking in, I felt like I should take my shoes off. The walls carried the scent of incense from hundreds of years of Masses sung with devotion; the air was pregnant with the sacred. As I entered the transept where the chapel is housed, my eyes were arrested by a series of paintings encircling the altar. Like an uncertain child taking a gift offered by a stranger, I approached them. One fresco in particular captured my imagination. This fresco was of Adam and Eve moments after being expelled from the garden. The expressions on their faces are excruciating. Her mouth agape with shock and horror, Eve's remorse is so palpable that it was impossible for me to look at her for very long.

"Who painted these?" I whispered.

Kenny stood behind me. "Masaccio, Lippi, and Masolino. Fourteenth century," he said.

He gave me space to take in the paintings.

"What do you think?" he asked after a few minutes.

"I feel like I'm standing inside the Bible."

Kenny nodded. "Like someone living in the Middle Ages," he said.

"What do you mean?"

"Medieval Europeans lived in a totally Christianized world. And they couldn't imagine it any other way," Kenny said.

I thought back to the clergy luncheon, and the speaker who'd railed about the powers of secularism driving Christianity out of the culture. "Times have changed," I said.

"That's why we have so much trouble understanding the medieval period. If you'd lived in the thirteenth century, your sense of time would be defined by the liturgical calendar. You'd see Bible stories everywhere—in paintings, statues, and stained-glass windows. At every Mass, you'd hear the tale of creation, fall, redemption, and re-creation in the liturgy. The ultimate metaphor was the grand cathedral located dead smack at the center of your town. The church and Christianity were the only game in town. They controlled the culture's stories," Kenny said.

"What would happen if you suggested another way of looking at things?" I asked.

"Like what?"

"Something other than what the Catholic Church taught."

Kenny laughed without humor. "You'd be burned at the stake," he said.

I rolled my eyes. "Nice," I said.

Kenny stepped down from the altar and sat in a pew, gesturing for me to sit next to him. We sat contentedly, letting the aesthetic force of the frescoes strike us head-on. There were twelve panels, each capturing a milestone moment from the Scriptures or Catholic tradition, mostly from the life of Peter—his preaching in Jerusalem, the death of Ananias, Peter healing the sick with his shadow, the raising of the son of Theophilus, Peter being freed from prison. Some were familiar to me; others Kenny pointed out. The chapel was awe-inspiring, but I wasn't sure why Kenny had brought me here.

He rested his arm on the back of the pew and faced me. "Chase, how do you feel about Catholicism?" he asked.

I smiled nervously. "I'm sorry?" I said.

"You make jokes about it—I'm just wondering what your feelings are," he said.

My initiation into conservative Christianity included being taught that Catholics weren't really "saved." People would say, "I'm trying to get my friend to visit our church." In a furtive tone, they would add, "He grew up Catholic." My misgivings about Catholicism were hard to slough off completely, and they left me feeling conflicted about Kenny. Here was a man I loved and respected—and yet . . .

"Well, I—"

Kenny, the masterful spiritual director, waited as I dangled on the end of my rope, searching for tactful words. He knew he had me in a catch-22.

"We're starting our pilgrimage in this chapel mainly to put the Catholic thing to rest," he said. "I don't want you pulling out the Catholic card every time Francis challenges you on something you don't want to look at."

I scanned the room. "OK, but why here?"

Kenny pointed at the frescoes. "To show you that Francis, you, and me—we share the same story," he said.

"Kenny—don't you think there's a big difference between what evangelicals and Catholics believe?" I asked.

"Oh, please—" he said.

"Are you ducking my question?" I asked.

"What do you want to talk about?" Kenny said. "Transubstantiation, sola scriptura versus the magisterium, praying to Mary, or all the other stuff Catholics and Protestants get hung up on? I'm too old for that. I'd rather be a reverent agnostic."

I widened one eye and narrowed the other. "You're an agnostic?" I asked.

"The word *agnostic* means 'not knowing.' There are countless mysteries that I have to stand before reverently and humbly while saying, 'I don't know,'" Kenny said.

"But what about our distinctives?"

"They're important too. But no one tradition has a corner on the faith market. Sharing the wisdom each of our traditions brings to the table will create more well-rounded Christians. Francis was a Catholic, an evangelical street preacher, a radical social activist, a contemplative who devoted hours to prayer, a mystic who had direct encounters with God, and someone who worshiped with all the enthusiasm and spontaneity of a Pentecostal. He was a wonderful integration of all the theological streams we have today," Kenny said.

"Can you envision Pat Robertson becoming a mystic?" I asked.

Kenny laughed. "Hard to imagine. But then again—God invented comedy."

I put my hands on the back of the pew in front of me and leaned forward, resting my chin on them. "It's strange to look at the Bible in a painting. I've always thought of it as a black-and-white photograph," I mused. "Everything in it had to be perfectly clear so no one could question it."

"How modern of you," Kenny said.

"What does that mean?"

"The medieval Christian perspective got beaten up during the Enlightenment. Enlightenment thinkers saw the universe less as a mystery and more as a machine where you got hold of truth by using reason, not divine revelation. The Christian worldview that had never been challenged before suddenly came under attack. Scientists replaced theologians, and the age of modernity was born."

"I'm sure that bugged some people," I said. I imagined groups of robed clerics wringing their hands and bemoaning their changed fortunes.

"Yes, eventually the church became so threatened by modernity's scorn that they turned the Bible into more of a history of ideas rather than a story."

"But why?"

"If they could make all their doctrines string together perfectly and logically, it would make the faith harder to discredit. But the Bible is less about ideas or doctrines than it is a story about people and their up-and-down relationships with God. It's—"

"More a painting than a photograph," I said.

"Right. It's not always clear, it's not black-and-white, you can't use it forensically in court, it's messy—and like all art it's open to many interpretations," Kenny said.

"So why do you say I'm a modern?" I asked.

Kenny paused. "Sometimes when you speak about your faith, you sound desperate and defensive, like you're afraid someone is going to come along and knock over all your blocks. That strips the poetry out of the Scriptures, out of following Jesus. I'm not surprised you woke up one day and asked yourself, 'Is this all there is?'"

"You want me to start thinking like I'm living in the Middle Ages?" I asked.

"Why not? Stop asking the painting to be a photograph. It's the *story* that makes sense of your life, and you don't need to apologize for choosing it," Kenny said. He stood up. "As a friend of mine used to say, the Bible is the story of how God gets back what was always his in the first place. People are looking for a story that can explain the way the world is. I think they're open to being romanced by the glory of the painting. I think Saint Francis can show us how to take advantage of the moment."

Kenny quickly looked at his watch. "We better hurry or we'll be late for our train to Assisi," he said.

I wasn't ready to leave so quickly. I turned to face the silent panels, to look at the story of stories—and something like hope mingled with wonder washed over me, deep inside. There, in the crowd, listening to Peter as he preached in Jerusalem; there walking beside Adam and Eve leaving Paradise; there standing in the background watching the death of Ananias—I saw myself. And for the first time in years, the enormousness of the Story burst forth like an expanding universe in my chest, and I was grateful it was mine.

IV

Start by doing what's necessary; then do what's possible;
and suddenly you are doing the impossible.

SAINT FRANCIS OF ASSISI

THE TWO-HOUR TRAIN RIDE FROM FLORENCE TO ASSISI TOOK SEV-eral hours. On the way, I caught the eye of an eighty-year-old, orthodontically challenged woman who noticed I wasn't wearing a wedding band. Like 90 percent of the old women in Italy, she wore black leather shoes with chunky heels. Her pilled, knee-high stockings had succumbed to the laws of gravity and bunched up around her ankles.

She apparently didn't feel the least bit embarrassed to be staring right at me with her toothless smile and her head nodding up and down like a dashboard bobblehead. After a few minutes, she crossed the aisle to where we were sitting and whispered something into Kenny's ear. His eyes widened, and he burst out laughing.

"What'd she say?" I asked.

"She thinks you're too skinny, and she wants you to come home with her so she can cook you a big meal," he answered.

"That's it?"

"She'd like you to meet her granddaughter too," he replied, wrapping his arms around her shoulder and hugging her while she giggled.

Getting off the train, Kenny and I jumped onto the public bus to make the journey up the winding road to the city of Assisi. From there, we were planning to walk down to the Chapel at

San Damiano. On the bus I learned an important survival tip—don't mess with Italian nuns. This particular species of religious is very high on the food chain. They are natural-born killers. I'd always thought of nuns as being sweet, mousy creatures who enjoyed playing old John Denver songs on folk guitars for grateful orphans. I was soon disabused of that stereotype. At our next stop, a gaggle of them were waiting in tight formation to board the bus. I should have realized something bad was about to happen because the locals who saw them through the windows began to shuffle around and murmur darkly, like nervous cows huddling together in an open field, anticipating a nasty squall. When the doors opened, the nuns made their charge. Determined to defy the laws of physics and make room for themselves, these black-habited assassins rushed in with their pointy elbows flying, their rulers whacking, and before I could smile and say, "*Buongiorno*," two of them had hip-checked me into the glass with such unbridled viciousness that I thought I was going to lose consciousness. To their credit, the old girls managed to carve out a space for themselves. I'm no longer surprised that the Catholic Church is one of the largest landholders in the world.

After all the excitement, I glanced through the driver's window and caught my first glimpse of the city some call "a particle of paradise." Assisi, wrapped in mist like a bride dressed in white. Perched on a spur on the western slope of Mount Subasio, Assisi pours down gently into the groves of olive trees that blanket her feet, leading to the verdant Spoleto Valley below. Above the city, the Rocca Maggiore fortress keeps a watchful eye on the city of Perugia, its former nemesis, sixteen miles across the open plain.

"Assisi's a small place," Kenny said from behind me. "It's seven-tenths of a mile long and three-tenths wide. In the medieval era, towns were built high up on hillsides so they'd be hard to attack. Being uphill, you could shoot arrows and pour boiling oil down on your enemy. And there was a second reason they were built on hillsides, having to do with sanitation and gravity. Even in ancient times, people figured out that 'you know what' runs downhill."

"It's incredible," I said, unable to take my eyes off it.

"Assisi's been given a lot of nicknames over the centuries. My favorite is, 'the doorway to God,'" Kenny said.

"Hope it's true," I said to no one in particular.

+ + +

Compared to the Church of Santa Maria del Carmine and the Brancacci Chapel, the Chapel of San Damiano was underwhelming. I'm not sure what I was expecting—certainly something with a little more bang for your buck than a simple oratory with a plain stone facade. I mean, come on—isn't this the place where Jesus told a guy to change the world? I was expecting something with a little more pizzazz. Anyone who's ever traveled to San Antonio to see the Alamo probably knows what I mean.

"Here's where it all began." Kenny closed his eyes and sighed. Thankfully he didn't pick up on my lack of enthusiasm, because his reverie was shattered by a great booming voice. From the portico that led into the side chapel, a rotund friar came bounding out, his arms spread wide in greeting. Given his considerable size, I was afraid he wouldn't be able to put the brakes on in time to avoid running us over. I was sure my being paralyzed by an overly exuberant friar would make an interesting segment for *Dateline NBC*.

"Brother Kenny!" he yelled. Behind him, two men walking with a little more dignity approached us as well.

"Bernard, what are you doing here? And look, Peter's with you!" Kenny cried. Bernard hoisted Kenny off the ground and spun him around like a rag doll. I'd never seen priests high-five before. It's a lot to take in all at once.

Brother Bernard had entered the Franciscan Order at the same time Kenny had. He was a Nebraska farm boy with hands the size of footballs. He was in his mid-fifties, yet despite his heft he looked much younger. Kenny and he had become fast friends while doing their doctoral programs at the Gregorian University in Rome. (In Catholic universities, a doctorate in theology is not referred to as a PhD but as an STD, Doctor of Sacred Theology. It's an unfortunate name for a degree. It must be hard for some-one's mother to say, "I'm so proud of my little boy. He went to seminary and got an STD.") Bernard's area of expertise was peace studies.

Brother Peter, three or four years older than me, was a for-mer Episcopal priest who had converted to Catholicism after a squabble with his bishop. He was from Charlottesville, Virginia, and spoke with the genteel cadence of a wealthy Southerner. He was completing his graduate work in liturgical studies at the Sant'Anselmo. Kenny had mentored him during his novitiate— his beginning first year.

They were quite the pair. Bernard looked like the character Hagrid, the gigantic groundskeeper in the Harry Potter movies, minus the beard. Peter was less effusive and seemed to enjoy play-ing the role of Bernard's kindly handler. Ruggedly handsome, I was sure his decision to live a celibate life was a grave disappoint-ment to women all across the European continent.

The third friar defied first impressions. At first it looked like he was purposely standing behind the corpulent Bernard so as not to be noticed. This wasn't hard to do. If someone parked a school bus behind Brother Bernard, you'd have had trouble seeing it.

There was an awkward silence while Kenny waited to be introduced to the diminutive stranger standing in Bernard's shadow, then Bernard remembered his manners. "Forgive me, forgive me," he exclaimed, breathing heavily (as a man who is at least seventy-five pounds overweight is apt to do). He stepped aside. "This is Brother Thomas."

Thomas slowly emerged from behind Bernard, and I was

gripped by a feeling I had never felt before and don't expect to again. He was a small man, maybe five foot four and a hundred pounds. His age was hard to peg, but if someone put a gun to my head, I'd have said he was in his early seventies. He was neither good-looking nor unattractive—if a friend asked you later to describe him, you'd be hard-pressed to find the right words. Instead, you'd describe how Thomas made you feel, because that's about the only thing you'd recall about him. Wisdom had placed her treasures in his soul for safekeeping. When he looked into your eyes, you swore he had known you in your mother's womb.

He shook my hand. "Hello," he said. For a moment no one else was there but him and me. He was sounding my depths; I could feel it in his hands.

"Brother Thomas, have we met before?" Kenny asked.

Bernard began, "Brother Thomas has an amazing story. He—"

"Let Thomas tell his own story," Peter said, gently elbowing Bernard.

"Years ago, I was a teacher of Franciscan spirituality and later a hermit," Thomas said. He sounded as if he were from somewhere in Eastern Europe.

"But now your vocation's changed?" Kenny said politely.

Thomas nodded. "People kept coming to my hermitage in the mountains to have me hear their confessions. Soon the Lord Jesus told me that being a hermit was too easy," he said, the corners of his mouth threatening to break into a grin. "He told me to become a traveling confessor. That's why I've come to Assisi," Thomas replied.

Kenny's eyes grew large. "I know who you are," he said. "I've heard stories about you."

Bernard couldn't contain himself. "Thomas has walked all over the world visiting shrines and hearing pilgrims make confessions."

"I'm so glad to meet you," Kenny said, shaking Thomas's hand.

"*Grazie*," Thomas replied.

Still holding Thomas's hand, Kenny gazed at him thoughtfully for a few seconds without speaking, then said, "When the student is ready the teacher appears. Perhaps you can tell my nephew the story of Francis and the Chapel of San Damiano."

"Of course," Thomas said, waving for us to follow him.

The interior of the Chapel at San Damiano is as unremarkable as the outside. Dark and musty, all the light in the sanctuary shines down from a rosette window set off center on the back wall. Leading us into the chapel, Brother Thomas walked down the center aisle between the austere wooden pews and pointed at the colorfully detailed Byzantine cross suspended by wires above the steps to the altar.

"After hearing the voice of Jesus from this cross, Francis came up with a plan for repairing this chapel. He would go door-to-door asking people to donate one stone each to rebuild the walls. Everyone thought he was crazy," Thomas said, pointing at his temple. "But it wasn't long before Francis's dream inspired everyone to pitch in. So much help came that Francis was able to renovate three churches."

Any preconception I'd had of hermits being reserved was vanishing. With every sentence, Thomas was becoming more and more animated. He paced back and forth, his speech becoming musical and rapturous. Soon he was nearly singing and dancing the San Damiano story. All of us were swept up in the tale, smiling at Thomas's growing excitement.

But there was one thing about the account that didn't make sense to me. "If Francis came from such a rich family, why didn't he just pay for the reconstruction himself? Wouldn't that have been easier?" I asked.

"Yes, yes, yes! Of course, that was his first thought as well," Thomas said. "Francis stole some of his father's most expensive cloth and sold it, along with his horse, to pay for the work.

His father, Pietro, was furious that his son was starting to be an embarrassment, so he dragged him before the local bishop to be punished for thievery.

"The whole town came out to watch the showdown between Francis and his father. Pietro told Bishop Guido that Francis should be banished from Assisi, but in the middle of his speech the crowd stopped listening to him and looked over at Francis. He'd quietly stripped off all of his clothes and was standing alone, stark naked."

Nearly whispering in his intensity, Thomas continued: "Francis walked over to his father and placed his clothes at his feet, along with the purse of money he'd received in return for the cloth and the horse, and said, 'Until today, I always called Pietro di Bernardone my father. From this day forward, I have only one father, my Father in heaven.' The bishop was so moved by Francis's saintliness that he stood up, took off his own cloak, and wrapped it around the young man's shoulders. Thus, Francis said farewell to his greedy father and his life as a young aristocrat. Now Francis was a true follower of our Lord Jesus. He had put off the old and put on the new. The camel had passed through the eye of the needle."

Silence descended on the room. Thomas briefly remained frozen like an aged Shakespearean actor in his last dramatic gesture —wound tight, looking energized by his telling of the story.

"Bravo! Well said, Brother Thomas!" Bernard thundered.

"You left out only one key point," Uncle Kenny said from two pews behind us. "Francis thought at the time that Jesus simply wanted him to rebuild a few chapels. He didn't yet realize how much more there was to it."

"Ah, yes," Thomas answered, reproving himself for not remembering to tell such an important part of the story. He looked at me and said, "As it turns out, Jesus was asking Francis to repair Christendom."

"Tall order," I said.

Thomas looked at me quizzically. Sarcasm is confusing to the pure of heart. "Yes, but he did it," he said.

We sat in the chapel and listened as Brother Thomas told us story after story about Francis. I pulled out my journal and tried to catch the highlights, hoping I could come back later and fill in the details. The waning Umbrian sun coming through the chapel windows told us that more time had passed than we had realized. We'd been with Brother Thomas for nearly three hours.

"Come spend the night with us at the San Rufino Friary. They have great food and an even better wine cellar," Brother Peter said, winking.

I was the last to leave the chapel. My impression of the place had changed. *True holiness is so often swaddled in the simple*, I thought. I paused and turned to have one last look at the figure of Jesus on the cross; I tried to imagine how Francis had felt, cutting all ties to his father to follow his Lord.

✝ ✝ ✝

On the drive to San Rufino, I prayed it would be just like the friary in Umberto Eco's *The Name of the Rose*. It didn't disappoint. Built in the early fourteenth century, the friary was an elaborate labyrinth of hallways, bedrooms, refectories, chapels, libraries, and mysterious rooms locked to prevent unwanted eyes from uncovering their secrets. I lived in delicious terror that if I wandered too far away from my companions I would get lost, only to be found years later, wandering the maze of dark passages with a great long beard, babbling incoherently.

We gathered for dinner on a stone veranda with unhindered views of the Apennines. Flickering candles crammed into wax-coated wine bottles threw arches of light against the wall behind us. I'd already figured out I would never meet a meal in Italy I wouldn't like. This one was simple but sublime. For starters,

Caprese (slabs of mozzarella cheese on top of succulent red toma-
toes with basil and fresh ground pepper), followed by carbonara
(pasta, egg, and pancetta, tossed in olive oil and peperoncini),
and a basket of new pears and apples for dessert. The dinner was
a gustatory miracle, but I kept glancing at my watch and waiting
for an opportune moment to excuse myself. Bernard, Peter, and
Kenny kept each other in fits of laughter as they recounted old
stories and caught up on all they'd been doing since they had last
seen each other. Thomas ate quietly, sometimes smiling and nodding. He seemed to enjoy watching old friends walk over long-
forgotten bridges together. I, on the other hand, was eager to do
some journaling.

I stood up and stretched. "If you men don't mind, I think I'll
take a walk and then go to bed," I said.

"Yes, yes, yes, see you in the morning," Bernard said, his chin
glistening with olive oil. I grabbed my backpack and walked
down the back stairs of the friary. I searched around until I found
a glade of grass high on a hill looking down on both the friary and
the city of Perugia. I pulled out my journal and began to write by
the light of the nearly full Umbrian moon.

Journal Entry:
Looking Out over Umbrian Plain

Dear Francis,

*If someone had told me a month ago that tonight I'd be sitting
under a full moon looking out over the Umbrian valley and writing a
letter to an 800-year-old saint, I'd have said they were crazy—and
yet here I am. Most of the time since arriving here I've felt out of it,
like I've taken too much Sudafed. Other times it's like an out-of-body
experience, like I'm in a theater watching a movie somebody else wrote
about my life. Kenny reminded me that I've been through a lot in
the last few weeks (if not the last two years!) and I need to be patient*

with myself. I'm praying I'll soon be more present to what's going on around me.

I've already gotten through one biography and several articles about you, and I still don't know if you were a genius, a lunatic, or both. Kenny says you were God's lover and that people who are in love should be forgiven for their excesses. Going out and asking people to donate stones for San Damiano was brilliant. It's a pretty incredible metaphor. I've been wondering what stones the church is going to need today to build a church that reaches postmodern people. It's going to take everyone bringing their own unique stone to get it done right.

I've been wondering whether in the beginning God wasn't rebuilding just San Damiano—he was also rebuilding you, Francis. Your life as a partier no longer satisfied. All your dreams of gaining glory as a knight were dashed. Your relationship with your father was finished. Wasn't your inner world a building that had fallen into disrepair? That's how I feel. I used to know what my "stone" was. I was the preacher, the "I got it all figured out" guy. Now I'm not so sure what I bring to the table, if anything.

I came across a great story about you called The Little Flowers *of St. Francis. I hope I can read it by flashlight. "One day when St. Francis was coming back from the woods, where he had been praying, and was at the edge of the forest, Brother Masseo went out to meet him, as he wanted to find out how humble he was, and he said to St. Francis, half jokingly, 'Why after you? Why after you? Why after you?'*

"St. Francis replied, 'What do you mean, Brother Masseo?'

" 'I mean, why does all the world seem to be running after you, and everyone seems to want to see you and hear you and obey you? You are not a handsome man. You do not have great learning or wisdom. You are not a nobleman. So why is all the world running after you?' "

That's the question I have for you, Francis. Why after you? Why did the world chase after you?

Pausing, I heard soft footsteps on the moist grass. I turned around, and there was Brother Thomas walking toward me.

Without a word, he sat cross-legged beside me. It's hard to sit in silence with someone you don't know very well. Instead, we turn to words to cover our inner nakedness. I once heard the Nobel Prize–winning author and Holocaust survivor Elie Wiesel say that in the art of writing it wasn't so much the actual words on the page that were important, but rather the tiny spaces between them. I think that means it isn't so much what the author says that matters, but what he chooses not to say. I'd never met anyone whose stillness spoke more powerfully than Thomas's. Grace emanated from him, and it brought consolation — but it was discomfiting as well. It was raw and kind, wild and motherly.

"Your uncle tells me you've come to Assisi on a pilgrimage," he said.

"I'm not sure what that means yet," I replied.

Thomas shrugged. "Don't worry. God will tell you when he's ready."

We sat and listened to the sounds of the night, the churring of insects whose names I don't know but whose songs always move me.

"Have you left your father yet?" Thomas asked.

"What?" I was jarred by his forwardness.

"Have you said good-bye to your father yet?"

I looked away from him. "I'm not sure what you mean," I said.

"I think you know," Thomas replied.

Under normal circumstances, I probably would have told him to mind his own business. But like the hemorrhaging woman in the gospels, I yearned to touch the hem of someone's cloak and pour out just a portion of my story at his feet.

I looked down between my knees and gave voice to my grief. "He hated that I wanted to go into ministry. He wanted me to be an investment banker, like he was. All he cared about was money and what it could buy — country clubs, big houses, and expensive cars. In his eyes, those were the things that made men great."

Someone had pressed the rewind button, and the door to a

room full of haunting memories creaked open. All the late-night arguments, the contempt in my father's eyes as I tried to explain my dreams to him, and my mother's ridiculous attempts to make peace between us.

"Do you want to be a prophet?" Thomas asked.

"What do you mean?"

"Everywhere I go, I meet people, old and young, from all over the world, and they tell me about their lives, their relationships, their broken families, their addictions, shame, guilt, failures. You'll never be able to speak into their souls unless you speak the truth about your own wounds. You need to tell them what Jesus has come to mean to you in the midst of your disappointments and losses. All ministry begins at the ragged edges of our own pain," he said.

I couldn't figure out how Thomas knew about my relationship with my father, much less that I was a pastor who was trying to fool people into believing he was perfect. For years I'd felt this pressure to convince everyone I had the leadership skills of Bill Hybels, the pastoral gifts of Henri Nouwen, and the teaching acumen of John Stott. I'd never thought sharing my brokenness with people was an effective church growth technique.

"Do you know the story of Rabbi Zusya?" Thomas asked. "He was a Chasidic master who lived in the 1700s. One day he said, 'When I get to the heavenly court, God will not ask me, "Why weren't you Moses?" Rather he will ask me, "Why were you not Zusya?"'"

Thomas let that thought hang in the air for a moment, then continued. "Churches should be places where people come to hear the story of God and to tell their own. That's how we find out how the two relate. Tell your story with all of its shadows and fog, so people can understand their own. They want a leader who's authentic, someone trying to figure out how to follow the

Lord Jesus in the joy and wreckage of life. They need you, not Moses," he said.

"I don't think I'm ready for that yet," I replied.

Thomas took my hand and squeezed it. "You will be," he said. "Do you know how Simon Tugwell described Franciscanism? He called it 'the radically unprotected life,' a life that's cruciform in shape," he said, opening his arms to mimic the posture of Jesus on the cross. "It's to live dangerously open, revealing all that we genuinely are, and receiving all the pain and sorrow the world will give back in return. It's to be real because we know the Real. Maybe living the unprotected life is what it means to be a Christian?"

I pondered this artful description of a follower of Jesus.

"How 'real' was Francis?" I asked.

"There was nothing false about him. He only knew how to be Francis, nothing more and nothing less. Do you know Thomas Aquinas?"

"Not well. I read some of the *Summa Theologica* in seminary, but it's been a long time."

"Aquinas spoke about two kinds of souls—the *magna animi* and the *pusilla animi*. The *magna animi* is the open soul that has space for the world to enter and find Jesus. It's where you get your word *magnanimous*. The *pusilla animi* is like that." He pointed at the dark outline of the Rocca Maggiore far up on the hillside, the fortress where the people of Assisi used to run when they were attacked by a neighboring city.

"The *pusilla animi* is the defended heart. It's a guarded and suspicious spirit that's closed to the world. It sees everything and everyone as a potential threat, an enemy waiting to attack. It shields itself from the world. It's where you get the word—"

"*Pusillanimous*," I said. "Someone who is fearful."

"Precisely. Francis possessed the *magna animi*. That's what each Christian, and the church, should be like."

I'm not sure how long I sat quietly, moving across the waters of Thomas's words.

"Thomas, why does it feel like God's abandoned me?" I asked at last.

Thomas sighed. "Sometimes God's presence is most strongly felt in his absence." He stood up and brushed the grass off his tunic. "Until tomorrow then?"

"Yes, tomorrow," I replied.

The evening air had taken a turn toward the cool side. Dressed in only a T-shirt and sandals, I was beginning to feel chilled. I thought Thomas had walked away, so I was startled when he came up behind me and gently wrapped his jacket around my shivering frame. He padded away, the sound of his steps obscured by the sound of the breeze moving across the valley and up the trees on the hillside.

As I thought about my father, the lights of Perugia became stars blurred in the distance, like the ones in Van Gogh's *Starry Night*.

"Good night, Dad," I said. It was a start.

V

The world is charged with the grandeur of God.
GERARD MANLEY HOPKINS

I SPENT THE MORNING RETURNING E-MAILS AT AN INTERNET CAFÉ
on the Via San Paolo. There were probably twenty-five messages
from folks back at Putnam Hill. Seven or eight of them began
with the words, "This morning in my quiet time, the Lord told
me to share this with you ..." Whenever another Christian says
they want to "share" something with you, it often means they're
about to blow your head off. Reading those e-mails was like being
beaten silly with a blunt object.

The rest, however, were touching. People wrote to say they
missed me and they were praying for me—and how much they
wanted me back. I was surprised I didn't beat myself up over the
painfully critical e-mails. I usually obsess about that kind of stuff.
Instead, I left the café with an odd sense of surrender. I knew it
wouldn't last, but for the moment I enjoyed it.

I returned to the friary and found the guys sitting in the common room reading the papers.

"*Buongiorno*," I said.

Kenny took off his reading glasses and put down his paper.
"So you're back. How was everything?" he asked with concern.

"I'm hanging in there," I replied.

Kenny stood up and stretched. "We have to run an errand.
Care to join us?"

"Sure. Where are we going?"

"Bernard needs to buy some altar supplies."

"Where does one 'buy' altar supplies?" I asked.

"At a clergy outfitters, of course," Bernard replied.

I laughed and threw up my hands. "Of course."

The store was just down the way from Saint Giacomo's Gate. Walking in was like entering a parallel universe: Jesus meets Rodeo Drive. Much of it was unfamiliar to me, but all I had to do was point, and someone chimed in with the appropriate label.

Mannequins dressed as cardinals in crimson capes and copes; shelves laden with gold chalices and crystal cruets for wine and water; racks of white linen albs; surplices with blousy, fluted sleeves; bishops' crosiers; stacks of prayer missals; glossy plaques of Pope Benedict; clerical shirts and collars; a thousand varieties of rosary beads; hermetically sealed cans filled with Communion hosts next to tins of incense and charcoal for thuribles. I kept thinking, *What on earth happens in these shops? Do priests stand in front of the mirror and ask the sales guy, "Does this chasuble make me look too fat? Or, "I'm not sure this cassock goes with my shoes. What do you think?" I imagined the store's tailor running back and forth with a tape measure draped around his neck, clapping his hands and yelling, "Accessorize, people, accessorize!"* If I had stayed any longer, my jaw would have suffered carpet burns.

"Ever been to a place like this before?" Peter asked.

"No," I whispered. "Do they sell indulgences to go?"

Peter took me by the elbow. "We should leave before you get us into trouble."

Bernard was in the checkout line while Kenny and Thomas were in the book section, poring over a new edition of *The Cloud of Unknowing*. "Gentlemen, I do believe it's time for us to move on," Peter announced in his best Virginia drawl. He peered out the store window. "It's too beautiful outside for us to be rummaging about inside," he said.

"What about a picnic at the Carceri?" Bernard called out.

"Can't you think of anything besides your stomach?" Peter asked.

"No," Bernard replied.

Thomas and Kenny met us by the front door. "Are you joining us, Brother Thomas?" Peter asked.

"Perhaps," Thomas said. "I have a friend at the hermitage. I may call him and come up later."

"We shouldn't be hard to find. Come, friends—to the refectory for provisions," Peter said, holding the door for us.

✝ ✝ ✝

The Carceri is a remote retreat snuggled high on Mount Subasio. Francis and the first friars went there for extended times of solitude and prayer. The word *carceri* actually means "prison," but it's a bit of a misnomer. If anything, the Carceri is enchanting. There's a fifteenth-century hermitage at the top where you can visit the Grotto of Saint Francis—the cave where Francis slept on a stone pillow for weeks at a time.

It took us two hours to climb to the peak. The serpentine road was lined with olive trees and yellow broom. Normally the trek takes only about an hour, but getting Bernard up the mountain was like pushing a grand piano up Mount Everest. Every ten minutes he'd have to stop, sit, and, of course, snack. Hiking with Pavarotti would have been easier.

There were lots of tourist groups and pilgrims wandering around, so Kenny took us off the beaten path to a grassy knoll that, apparently, few people knew about. The air was lightly scented with rosemary and lavender. Peter laid out a feast of sandwiches filled with Italian meats, provolone, and, of course, more Umbrian wine.

"Let's use the 'Canticle' to say grace," Bernard suggested. I was surprised he wanted to do anything that would delay the meal.

"It's a bit long," Peter replied, but Bernard had already started.

Most high, all powerful, all good, Lord!
All praise is yours, all glory, all honour
And all blessing.

To you, alone, Most High, do they belong.
No mortal lips are worthy
To pronounce your name.

All praise be yours, my Lord, through all that you
   have made,
And first my lord Brother Sun,
Who brings the day; and light you give to us through him.
How beautiful is he, how radiant in all his splendour!
Of you, Most High, he bears the likeness.

All praise be yours, my Lord, through Sister Moon
   and Stars;
In the heavens you have made them, bright
And precious and fair.

All praise be yours, my Lord, through Brothers Wind
   and Air,
And fair and stormy, all the weather's moods,
By which you cherish all that you have made.

All praise be yours, my Lord, through Sister Water,
So useful, lowly, precious and pure.

All praise be yours, my Lord, through Brother Fire,
Through whom you brighten up the night.
How beautiful is he, how gay! Full of power and strength.

All praise be yours, my Lord, through Sister Earth,
   our mother,
Who feeds us in her sovereignty and produces
Various fruits with coloured flowers and herbs.

All praise be yours, my Lord, through those who
   grant pardon
For love of you; through those who endure

Sickness and trial.
Happy those who endure in peace,
By you, Most High, they will be crowned.

All praise be yours, my Lord, through Sister Death,
From whose embrace no mortal can escape.
Woe to those who die in mortal sin!
Happy those she finds doing your will!
The second death can do no harm to them.

Praise and bless my Lord, and give him thanks,
And serve him with great humility.

Without skipping a beat, the three of them signed themselves with the cross, said "Amen," and began passing around the food.

"Whoa, you guys! What on earth was that?" I asked.

"What on earth was what?" Kenny replied, looking around to see if something was sneaking up on us.

"That prayer!"

Kenny relaxed and smiled. "That's not a prayer. It's a poem by Francis called 'Canticle of the Creatures.' You didn't study it in college?" he asked.

"No," I said, feeling foolish. I'd majored in English and Romance language.

Kenny laughed. "You might want to ask for your money back. It's the earliest poem we have in the Italian vernacular. Bernard, could you pass me the butter?"

I poured the Sagrantino di Montefalco into plastic cups and passed them around. The deep pomegranate red wine released a delicate fragrance of violet and rose. "So Francis was a big nature lover?" I asked.

"More than just a nature lover, he was the first Christian environmentalist," Kenny said.

"He's the patron saint of ecology," Bernard added.

"Kenny, Francis was clearly more than an environmentalist,"

Peter insisted. "He was a nature mystic. His love for the earth shaped his whole theology." Peter turned to me. "Franciscans call it a 'spirituality of creation,'" he said.

"Spirituality of creation?" I asked.

"Have you ever heard of the 'Great Chain of Being'?" Kenny asked.

"Is it the name of a band?"

The three of them chuckled. "Hardly," Kenny said. "The Great Chain of Being was something that theologians known as the Scholastics came up with in the Middle Ages. They said the world was a place where God, angels, human beings, animals, plants, rocks, minerals, water, and the earth itself were all bound together. Each part of the chain related interdependently with all the others in a logical way and together bore witness to God's glory and beauty."

Bernard jumped in. "They saw the whole thing as a cosmic symphony."

"Francis took this idea one step further," Peter said. "He believed everything we see in creation is a reflection of the Creator, just as we are. Francis treated everything in creation as if it were his brother or sister, because we all have the same Parent."

"So Francis was a *pantheist*," I said.

"No!" they yelled in unison.

"A pantheist," Peter said, "is someone who believes that God and the creation are one and the same thing. Francis didn't worship God *as* creation; he worshiped God *through* creation. For him, the world was a prayer book where the *vestigia Dei*, the footprints of God, could be found everywhere."

Bernard reached into his backpack and pulled out a weather-beaten book. "This is the first biography written about Saint Francis — *The Second Life of Saint Francis* by Thomas of Celano. I carry it everywhere," he said, thumbing through it frantically in search of something. Then he held up his index finger. "One of my favorite passages."

> In every work of the artist he praised the Artist; whatever he found in the things made he referred to the Maker. He rejoiced in all the works of the hands of the Lord and saw behind things pleasant to behold their life-giving reason and cause. In beautiful things he saw Beauty itself; all things were to him good. 'He who made us is the best,' they cried out to him. Through his footprints impressed upon things he followed the Beloved everywhere; he made for himself from all things a ladder by which to come even to his throne.
>
> He embraced all things with a rapture of unheard of devotion, speaking to them of the Lord and admonishing them to praise him. He spared lights, lamps, and candles, not wishing to extinguish their brightness with his hand, for he regarded them as a symbol of Eternal Light. He walked reverently upon stones, because of him who was called the Rock ...
>
> He forbade the brothers to cut down the whole tree when they cut wood, so that it might have hope of sprouting again. He commanded the gardener to leave the border around the garden undug, so that in their proper times the greenness of the grass and the beauty of flowers might announce the beauty of the Father of all things.

Bernard finished reading and we sat in silence. The mist that had covered the valley earlier in the day had disappeared. Visible in the distance were acres and acres of sunflowers, whose blooms turn to follow the sun's warmth throughout the course of the day. The Spoleto plains lay like a fecund ocean of green. How would Francis have seen this vista differently than I did?

I sat up on my knees. "OK, but what about the stories of Francis talking to animals? Do you believe them?" I asked.

In every book I'd read about Francis, there were stories I

immediately relegated to the Doctor Doolittle myth pile. For instance, in one story Francis saved a town called Gubbio from a wolf by negotiating a peace treaty between them. Years later, when the wolf died, the whole town went into mourning because they'd all become such good friends. In another story, Francis tamed turtledoves in Siena that ended up becoming members of his order. He removed worms from walking paths so people wouldn't step on them, and convinced crickets to pray with him. In another account, a group of sheep grazing in a field saw him walking down the road and ran to receive a blessing from him. Before you know it, they were all singing hymns together. And then there's the story of the lamb Francis adopted that would genuflect every time they had Communion.

I've met people who claimed they could talk to animals—most of these folks were pretty heavily medicated.

"Do you know the story of Francis preaching to the birds?" Peter asked.

I lay down on my side and propped my head on my hand. "Can't say I've heard that one," I said.

Peter pointed down the hill. "People say it happened by that bridge over there. One day as Francis was walking with a group of friars, he saw a huge flock of crows and doves at the base of a big holm oak. When he ran down to greet them, none of them flew away; they could tell Francis was different from other people. So he gathered them all together and began to preach to them."

Peter stood up, cleared his throat, and performed an improvised version of Francis's sermon. "My brother birds, make a point of always praising the Creator. He clothed you in feathers and gave you wings to fly in the kingdom of the air. Remember that no matter what happens, he will provide for you, even though you don't know how to sow or reap. So worry for nothing, and rejoice in the One who made you."

"So what happened?" I asked, somewhat impressed.

"The birds stretched out their necks, flapped their wings with delight, and refused to leave until he'd made the sign of the cross over each of them," Peter said.

Just as Peter finished, Bernard jumped in and read from his book again:

> After the birds had listened so reverently to the word of God, he began to accuse himself of negligence because he had not preached to them before. From that day on, he carefully exhorted all birds, all animals, all reptiles, and also insensible creatures, to love the Creator, because daily, invoking the name of the Savior, he observed their obedience in his own experience.

"And you buy this?" I asked.

Kenny smiled and shrugged. "Jesus instructed the disciples to 'go into all the world and proclaim the gospel to the whole creation.' Francis took those words literally. Francis knew it wasn't just people who were waiting in anticipation for creation to be liberated from sin, but the entire Great Chain of Being as well. Most Christians don't think about that. We think we're the center of the universe, and that God is only interested in saving individual souls rather than all of creation. The condition of the earth would be a lot different today if Christians saw the world as Francis did."

"Meaning we'd have taken better care of it?" I asked.

Kenny nodded. "Unlike animals, we're endowed with reason. That gift comes with a God-given responsibility to care for creation. It's pretty obvious that Christians have dropped this ball in a really big way. You know in Genesis where it says that the Lord put us in the garden to work and take care of it?"

"Sure," I said.

Kenny continued, "The word *work* in Hebrew is *abad*, and it means 'to serve,' to be a servant to creation. The word for 'to take care of' is *shamar*, and It implies watchful care and preservation.

We allowed these texts to be twisted so that *dominion* came to mean 'domination,' and *stewardship* came to mean 'exploitation.' The problem is, once you damage or break just one of the links in the Great Chain of Being, the whole is affected. Everything in the natural world is connected. If we destroy it, we destroy ourselves."

"It's sad that we've made this into just a political issue when, in fact, it's theological as well," Peter added. "If we continue allowing the earth to be destroyed, we're actually working against the purposes of Jesus, who died for it."

I was embarrassed by how little I'd thought about the relationship between my faith and the natural world. I wouldn't have put caring for the environment in the same category as witnessing or Bible study.

Peter glanced at his watch and jumped up. "Bernard, Kenny— look at the time," he said.

Bernard stood up and brushed the crumbs off his habit. "Oh, dear," he said.

"We only have thirty minutes to get back for evening prayer," Kenny said.

The three men sprang into action, stuffing the remains of the picnic into their backpacks. They scurried about as if some distant sentry had just sounded an alarm warning that pagan hordes were at the city gates.

While the three of them scrambled to get everything together, I noticed Thomas coming down the hermitage steps with another friar, both of them holding up their habits so they wouldn't trip. Thomas looked very pleased with himself.

"Were you able to do it?" Peter called as Thomas approached.

"Do what?" I asked.

Thomas and his companion joined our group, and Thomas beamed at me. "I persuaded the guardian of the hermitage to let you spend the night in one of the caves," he said.

I swallowed hard. "You want me to spend the night in one of these caves?"

Thomas nodded enthusiastically. "Yes," he said.

I love the outdoors, but I'd never been big on the whole camping thing. My idea of roughing it was staying in a hotel without HBO. "Brother Thomas, I really appreciate the offer, but—"

"Can I speak to our friend alone for a moment?" Peter interrupted, placing his arm around my shoulders.

"Of course," they said. Bernard quickly engaged Thomas and the other friar in conversation while Peter pulled me out of earshot.

"Being granted permission to spend the night in one of the caves at the Carceri is a *very, very* big deal. How Thomas got the guardian to let you stay here is beyond me. If you say no to staying here tonight, Thomas will be crushed," he said.

The last thing in the world I wanted to do was wound Thomas. "All right," I said, resignedly.

Relief washed across Peter's face. "Thank you," he said, then cleared his throat to get everyone's attention. "Chase says it would be an honor to spend the night in the caves. He's very grateful, aren't you, Chase?" he said, poking me in the back.

"Absolutely," I said, smiling.

✝ ✝ ✝

Thomas had thought ahead. He'd brought my backpack with my journal, Bible, and a handful of other books inside. Before leaving, the guardian gave me a candle, some bread and cheese, a thermos of water, and a musty old blanket. "This should keep you until morning," he said cheerily in heavily accented English. "Let me show you the cave."

Saying good-bye, Thomas, Bernard, Peter, and Kenny promised to collect me first thing in the morning. Peter winked and gave me two thumbs up.

The cave was smaller than I'd expected. The walls were shiny and smooth, as if millions of pilgrims' hands had reverently stroked them over hundreds of years. I joined mine with theirs, feeling my way along the cold stone in search of a place to sleep later on. Against one wall was a place to kneel, in front of which a crucifix was hung, attached to the cave's wall with a large, rusty nail and old, twisted wire. After spreading my blanket, I sat at the cave's entrance. I looked down on the valley below, bathed in the last shadows of twilight, and thought about how far away Putnam Hill was. The trees whispered, and I heard the soft sounds of creatures burrowing about in search of shelter. I heard the call of an owl keeping watch over the coming night, waiting for small prey to peek out, revealing hidden nesting places.

"How did I get here?" I asked the moon. The question had little to do with locale. Only the leaves answered. The stars were coming out, and the sky was so dark that I could see the Milky Way, something I hadn't seen since I was a boy at summer camp in Maine. The sky in Thackeray was usually too full of ambient light from New York City to see the full canopy of the heavens that most in Umbria took for granted.

It had been a long time since I had sat in silence with the cosmos. At first it was unsettling, if not terrifying, to be alone with the Alone, but after a while I fell into the arms of stillness. I pulled out my journal and the stub of a pencil and huddled next to my candle, hoping to sketch the valley from memory. I tried to capture mulberry trees, knotted oaks, the gleaming fields. Finally it was dark, and I picked up my pen and turned to writing instead.

Journal Entry:
The Carceri

Dear Francis,

I remember as a kid growing up playing in the woods behind our house. How many times did I go there when Dad was going

*through one of his bad spells? One day when I was around 11, I was
walking there when out of the blue I felt like I wasn't alone. God was
everywhere, and I knew he understood how lonely and despairing I was.
In that wild place, I heard his voice say that one day things would be
better. When did I lose that childlike ability to hear God in nature?*

*Kenny made me read this thirteenth-century Franciscan theologian
named Dun Scotus, who said we shouldn't talk about things in the
created order in universal terms but only in the specific. God didn't
create species or genus as much as individuated expressions of himself.
As Richard Rohr says, all things are endowed with "this-ness." It's this
oak, this tulip, this dog. A personal, unique God makes a personal,
unique creation. Maybe if we saw the particularity of all living things,
we'd treat the world with more reverence and awe. In their this-ness, all
created things are uniquely sacred. You believed that.*

*There's this great old hymn from the turn of the previous century
called "This Is My Father's World." We sing it at my church all the
time. I think you'd love it.*

> *This is my Father's world, and to my listening ears*
> *All nature sings, and 'round me rings the music of the spheres.*
> *This is my Father's world: I rest me in the thought*
> *Of rocks and trees, of skies and seas;*
> *His hand the wonders wrought.*
>
> *This is my Father's world, the birds their carols raise,*
> *The morning light, the lily white, declare their Maker's praise.*
> *This is my Father's world: He shines in all that's fair;*
> *In the rustling grass I hear Him pass, He speaks to me everywhere.*

*Can you believe I've sung that hymn a million times and never once
stopped to consider what it was saying?*

I don't know how long I sat outside that cave, straining to hear
the music of the spheres that Francis heard. Eventually, I shook my
head and laughed at myself. How could I believe it was possible to
manufacture an event that the mystics and hermits of old waited

lifetimes to experience? Living in deserts or wilderness, they cried out to God, "Just once! Just once! Let me hear it but once!" while I sit outside a grotto for twenty minutes praying, "Right now! Right now!"

I picked up my backpack and put my journal and pen away. On the bottom of the bag I felt a folded piece of paper. It was a note written on the back of a receipt. No explanation—just two quotes scribbled in a hurry:

Dearest Chase,

"The best remedy for those who are afraid, lonely, or unhappy is to go outside, somewhere where they can be quiet, alone with the heavens, nature, and God. Because only then does one feel that all is as it should be and that God wishes to see people happy, amidst the simple beauty of nature."—Anne Frank

"If a man walks in the woods for love of them half of each day, he is in danger of being regarded as a loafer. But if he spends his days as a speculator, shearing off those woods and making the earth bald before her time, he is deemed an industrious and enterprising citizen."—Henry David Thoreau

> *Pax et Bonum,*
> *Thomas*

Getting up, I took my candle and went back into the cave. Even though I was exhausted, I knelt in front of the crucifix, and the words of David in Psalm 8 came to me: "When I consider your heavens, the work of your fingers, the moon and the stars, which you have set in place, what is mankind that you are mindful of them, human beings that you care for them?" And my soul was gladdened.

VI

The Christian of tomorrow will be a mystic,
one who has experienced something,
or he will be nothing.

KARL RAHNER

TWO DAYS LATER, BACK AT THE FRIARY IN ASSISI, KENNY MADE A
surprise announcement—he was going to Siena for a retreat with
aspirants interested in joining the order.

"What do you mean you're going to Siena? What am I supposed to do while you're gone?" I asked, looking out his bedroom
window at the dark rain clouds frowning on the horizon.

Kenny threw some clothes into a leather overnight bag. "Don't
worry, you're in good hands. Bernard won't let you go hungry."
That I hadn't slept well the night before wasn't helping matters. I
had tossed in bed for hours, rehearsing my last meeting with the
elders again and again until the sun shot through the slats on my
wooden blinds. I couldn't shake Ed's last words to me. They tore
open a fissure in my soul from which torrents of shame and guilt
were running.

Kenny placed his hand on my shoulder. "Get into the rhythm
of the friary. Go to morning and evening prayer; walk the grounds;
get to know the others. I'll be back in a few days, and I'm sure
you'll have all kinds of interesting things to report."

I peered through the curtains on the refectory window as
Kenny's car pulled out of the gravel drive and disappeared around
a sharp bend in the road. I remembered my parents dropping
me off at summer camp every year. I'd stand in the parking lot

watching their taillights fade into the distance, wishing I could be anywhere but where I was.

In the end, I resigned myself to Kenny's departure and made the best of the two rainy days that followed. I passed long hours sitting in the friary's library, reading books on the life of Saint Francis and Franciscan spirituality. On second thought, *library* might be too grandiose a term. The room contained four bookshelves made of coarse plywood and filled with musty tomes about Francis. A nonagenarian friar whose breath could have knocked a buzzard off a manure wagon at thirty yards guarded the collection jealously. Old Brother Leo spent the better part of every day sitting in a tired lumpy chair strategically stationed between the fireplace and the bookshelves. Despite his failing faculties, Brother Leo was revered by the other friars, as well as by all of Assisi. During the war, he'd hidden Jewish children in the friary's wine cellar and spent three years in a concentration camp for it. The guardian of the friary had decided that being the house's librarian was an honorable way for Brother Leo to pass his autumn years. Whenever I went back to get a new book, I would have to perform what I affectionately came to call "the Litany of Brother Leo."

"Here I am, Brother Leo," I would announce as I entered the library.

"Did you bring the other book back?" he'd ask gruffly, eyes at half-mast.

"Yes, Brother Leo," I'd say respectfully.

"The world is full of thieves," he'd mutter irritably. And with that he would slowly slip back into the ether of an old man's dreams.

Every morning I avoided having to go to Mass, even though Brother Bernard did everything he could to persuade me to join them. On Thursday I slipped out and went for a long walk, knowing he would come to my bedroom to invite me. On Friday I feigned a stomachache. On Saturday I developed a brain tumor. I was running out of excuses.

I'm not sure what I was so afraid of. It's not like I'm a member of a radical fringe group who thinks the Catholic Church is apostate. I think I was nervous about missing all the liturgical cues and looking like an idiot. I was terrified that when the congregation stood up, I'd sit down. When they sat down, I'd stand up. When they knelt, I would probably lie down. More than anything else, I was afraid that messing up the choreography would prove to everyone I was an outsider, a feeling I knew all too well. More important, I just wasn't ready for church yet, Catholic or otherwise. Even though medieval churches couldn't be more different from Putnam Hill, I didn't want to revisit a God-space that reminded me of my fall from grace. I was afraid that if I went to church, God would look at me under his microscope and tell the world I'd been found lacking.

On Sunday morning, however, there was no escaping. Bernard cornered me in the hallway bathroom and asked if I would join him and the others for an espresso at a café on Corso Mazzini. Like a dope I said sure, not stopping to consider what day it was and that friars probably had a standing appointment with God. I knew I was in trouble when Bernard stepped on the gas and flew past the café where we were supposed to stop. I looked out the rear window at the street-side tables fading in the distance.

"Where are we going?" I asked.

"Don't worry." Bernard said. I heard the car doors locking and Peter tittering. Thomas never said a word.

Three blocks later, we pulled up in front of the Chiesa Nuova. Italians venerate this church because it's built over the home where Francis was born, and where his father had his cloth shop.

Bernard shut off the engine and looked at me in the rearview mirror. "Ready for church?"

Before I could voice my objections, Bernard got out of the car and offered me his arm. I'd been ambushed by friars.

The church was filled with worshipers. Some gazed adoringly at the crucifix above the altar; others fingered rosary beads, eyes closed and lips moving silently in prayer. In a corner at the front, left-hand side of the chapel was a cell carved into the wall with a life-size statue of Francis behind bars, praying on his knees.

"That's where Francis's father locked him up after his conversion," Peter whispered.

"Sort of the medieval version of being grounded?" I asked.

Peter shook his head and ushered me into a pew. "Something like that," he said.

Despite my reservations, the Mass turned out to be beautiful, filled with pageantry and solemnity. The priest entered in a cloud of incense, and his voice resounded through the sanctuary with an unearthly authority. Peter handed me a booklet with an English translation of the liturgy so I could follow along. Much of the liturgy for the Mass, filled with its formularies, prayers, and creeds, is well over a thousand years old. I was moved that people were offering up the same words, giving expression to the same truths in different languages and time zones all around the globe that very day. Some were singing the liturgy in grand cathedrals in Europe, and some under a lush canopy of trees in Africa. Some were performing the liturgy in secret house churches in China, and others in prison chapels. Where or how it was said didn't matter. Solidarity mattered.

As I pondered the faces of saints captured in stained glass, the frescoes that adorned the walls and ceilings of the nave and apse, it dawned on me that the liturgy was connecting me to a long and ancient line of believers. Time had become irrelevant. We were one chorus, one communion of saints. I was but one soul in the long procession of the faithful that wound its way down and along the hilly landscape of history. I was appropriately small.

When the time came for people to go forward to receive the Eucharist, I was gripped by panic.

"Come join us," Bernard whispered.

I gazed at the floor and shook my head. "I can't," I said.

"No one will know you're not a Catholic," he said.

"It's not that." I looked around to see if anyone was listening in on our conversation. "I just can't right now," I said.

Bernard looked at me tenderly and patted my shoulder. When he reached the end of the pew, he looked back to see if I had changed my mind and then melted into the stream of the faithful making their way to the altar. Suddenly a feeling that I'd long tried to keep at bay found a breach in my battered defenses and overtook me. All my life, I'd felt like a kid standing outside a house, nose pressed against a window, looking in at a roomful of people having a party. I'd spent years waving and tapping on the glass, hoping they'd finally see me and invite me in. I'd gone to a great college; I'd worked hard at being a "good Christian"; and I was the founding pastor of a successful church. What more did the world want from me before it offered me the gift of belonging?

Aloneness wrapped itself around my chest so tightly that I could barely breathe. My soul's descent into despair was slowed by the sound of hard-soled shoes shuffling along the marble floor behind me. I turned to see a very old man being helped to the altar by two others—*Probably his grandsons*, I thought. He reminded me of a mortally wounded soldier being carried off the battlefield to a first-aid station. At the altar rail, he impatiently shrugged off the hands of his caretakers and fell to his knees, rasping for air. When he extended his hands to receive Communion, my heart crumpled with sadness. I was as hungry, hobbled, and desperate for God as this old man, yet my sense of unworthiness riveted me to the pew. Even though Jesus beckoned me and I yearned for him, I could no more go to that altar rail than jump across the Grand Canyon. I bowed my head and wept until my ribs ached.

Bernard and Thomas returned and sat on either side of me. They made no attempt to assuage my grief. They were sentries, guarding my solitude.

I wiped my eyes and realized that Peter hadn't returned from receiving Communion. I peered around the end of the pew and there he was, lying prostrate on the floor before the altar, his arms outstretched and his face turned to one side, serene and prayerful.

I looked at Bernard. "Is something wrong?" I asked.

Bernard stood halfway to catch a glimpse of what I was seeing. He shrugged. "No," he said.

I was relieved when the priest declared that the Mass was over and that we should go in peace. Bernard, Thomas, and I walked down the aisle of the church into the late-morning Umbrian sunlight, leaving Peter behind. I struggled to find words to explain why I'd lost my composure, but as I was about to speak, Thomas squeezed my hand. "Not to worry; sometimes prayers are wet," he said.

✝ ✝ ✝

Riposo is to the Italians what *siesta* is to the Spanish. Every day between one and four o'clock, entire cities shut down so people can go home to eat the main meal of the day with their families and rest before returning to work. So what that the Italians aren't a superpower? After two weeks in Italy, I decided that, given the choice between taking a nap every afternoon and ruling the planet, I'd choose the former.

After my experience in the church, I needed a *riposo* in the worst of ways. I was deep in REM sleep when I heard a knock on my door. It was Sister Raisa, an elderly nun from Latvia who worked in the refectory.

"Mr. Falcon, there is a phone call for you," she said. Sister Raisa is sweet, but not real good with names. I walked out into the hallway, licked my hands, and tried to pat down my hair. A few doors down, I saw Kenny standing at the door to his room juggling luggage, packages, and keys.

I stopped to hug him. "Boy, am I glad to see you. Are you just getting back? How was Siena?" I asked.

Kenny smiled. "Wonderful. Did I hear you have a call?" he asked, smiling and nodding to Sister Raisa.

I frowned. "Yeah. Hope it's not the ax falling."

Kenny finally got his door open, but not before dropping half his stuff. "I'll be here if you need me, OK?" he said, bending over to pick up his things.

I followed Sister Raisa down the stairs to the main office of the friary. We walked through the reception area and into the guardian's study. Books and papers were piled on every available flat surface.

"Looks like the Catholics need a patron saint of clutter," I said, stepping over a pile of books. Sister Raisa smiled in a confused sort of way and pointed to the phone on the guardian's desk.

"Hello?"

"Chase, it's Maggie."

I collapsed into the desk chair. "Maggie? How'd you get this number?"

"I went to the church office and got it out of Lucinda, the receptionist," she answered. Maggie once spent six months in jail for drug possession; Lucinda hadn't had a prayer.

"How are you?" she asked.

"I wouldn't even know where to start," I said. "How's everything at home?"

"Chip preached today," she said.

I swiveled around and stared out the window behind the desk. "How'd he do?" I asked.

"I think he got it from sermons-r-us.com." I could almost hear Maggie's eyes rolling. "Chase, I'm using a phone card so I only have a few minutes. The church is freaking out," she said.

My heart skipped a beat. "What's happening?" I asked.

"There's one group of people who say you shouldn't be allowed to come back no matter what. Then there's another group who think you deserve another chance and want you home as soon as possible. Coffee hour was a bloodbath," Maggie said.

"Oh, no," I said. "What else?"

"If you talk to Chip, watch your back."

"What?"

"He wants your job," Maggie said.

I sat upright. "You're kidding, right?"

"Don't write him off. Lots of people are loving on him, and he seems to be enjoying the attention," Maggie replied.

"Thanks for the advice," I said. I paused for a moment. "How are *you* doing, Maggie?" I asked. It had been only a few weeks since Iris's funeral.

Maggie sighed. "My AA sponsor says grieving is like walking in molasses; you plow through it one step at a time. I'm still holding on to God, though," she said.

My throat knotted. "Still?"

"Still," she replied.

I shot a prayer of thanks toward the ceiling. "Thanks again for the heads-up on Chip. If he calls, I promise not to say anything that could be used against me in a court of law."

"Can I call again?" Maggie asked.

"I'd love it, but next time call from a number I can call you back on."

"Hang in there," she said and hung up.

✝ ✝ ✝

Time in Italy has a different symmetry. Days came and went, drawing little attention to themselves; sometimes I couldn't say if it was Tuesday or Friday. I took walks, ate, spent time with Kenny or one of the guys, and read and wrote in my journal. The deeper

I plunged into the heart of Francis, the more courage I found to dive into my own. The more I saw his love for the church and the world, the more inspired I was to follow his lead. I was defrosting.

During the last week of April, the mood in Assisi changed as the city ramped up for Calendimaggio — a wild three-day festival celebrating the return of spring and the victory of life over death. The festival's roots go back to the Middle Ages, when two rival families and their supporters were locked in a long, bloody struggle to control the city. Today, the competition between the *Sopra* (the upper part of the city) and the *Sotto* (the lower part) is a little more peaceful. Now the festival revolves around a competition of song, theater, dance, and processions. The Assisiani live for these three days, so no expense is spared — stages are erected all over the city; the streets are festooned with colorful flags; musicians and jugglers vie for room on every corner; and all the restaurants serve the traditional meal of pork and wine. Two days before the festival officially began, people were already flooding into the city. I was sitting on the friary steps, listening to the conversations of passing tourists and trying to guess their home country, when Peter came out and sat next to me.

"Care to go into town and see what's happening?" he asked.

"Where do you want to go?"

"Let's grab a *limoncello* and people-watch by the fountain."

As we walked to the Piazza del Comune, it dawned on me that Assisi is a town of smells, bells, and birds. Everywhere, packs of pigeons strut about pecking crumbs from between cobblestones. Frightened by sound or step, they fly off, swooping in grand circles around spires and domes. The air is filled with the scent of wood fires from ovens baking pizzas for hungry tourists, while every fifteen minutes the hours are named by the ringing of bells in belfries across the city.

Peter and I bought two limoncellos, a bittersweet citrus liqueur, and sat on the steps of the fountain facing the Temple of Minerva. I used to think New England had old buildings, but Italy's got us licked. The Minerva was built by the Romans in the first century and then dedicated to the twin gods of Castor and Pollux. Its six channeled columns with Corinthian capitals stand nobly, effortlessly holding up history. The whole town makes you feel like you can trust eternity. So much has gone before us that surely there must be something waiting for us on the other side of it.

The day had steadily become warmer, so we stretched our legs, closed our eyes, and pointed our faces toward the sun. We were quiet a long time before I spoke. "Church was pretty crazy the other day," I said.

Peter didn't move. "How so?" he answered.

"I guess you could say I was overwhelmed by it."

Peter shielded his eyes against the sun with his hand and squinted at me. "And you're not sure why?" he asked.

I nodded.

He took a deep breath and let it out. "It's complicated," he said.

"Try me."

Sitting up, Peter took a sip of his limoncello and gathered his thoughts. "First tell me what you think happened," he said.

I leaned my back against the base of the fountain. "Part of me wants to write it off as a reaction to everything that's happened in the last three weeks, but saying it was just a cathartic meltdown sounds too cynical to me," I said.

Peter laughed. "Retrace your steps. What was it like when you walked into the church?"

I picked up small bits of marble and flicked them into the street while I thought about an answer. "It was like I was walking into another world."

"Precisely. Medievals built huge ornate churches so that people walking into them would feel like they'd left one world and entered another reality—the kingdom of God. Think of what happened to your senses when you came in those doors. Stained-glass windows, frescoes and paintings, dimmed lights, flickering candles, the smell of incense, vaults and arches pulling your spirit upward, angels soaring on the ceilings. God snuck up on you through the architecture," Peter said.

"You mean the building spoke to me?" I asked.

Peter nodded. "Augustine said the human mind was particularly delighted when truth was presented to it indirectly, like in symbols and sacred space. Unfortunately, most churches today are designed without any sense of the iconic because moderns like straightforward, unambiguous communication. We want 'worship centers' where hominess is more important than holiness."

I'd forgotten that Peter was a doctoral candidate in liturgics. He spoke so convincingly that it was hard for me not to feel some measure of embarrassment. When we designed Putnam Hill, we focused on the utilitarian more than anything else. I remember telling our architect that I wanted all the technological goodies you'd find in a world-class performing arts center. Looking back, I realize that what I had asked for was "lights, camera, action!" rather than "Father, Son, and Holy Ghost."

"Anything else beside sacred space?" I asked.

Peter leaned toward me like he wanted to tell me a secret. "Next come the liturgy and the Eucharist," he replied.

Now we were getting into the spooky stuff. When we started Putnam Hill, we downplayed the Communion thing because it didn't fit into our seeker-sensitive paradigm. We have it once a quarter, but it's kind of like eating broccoli—we don't particularly enjoy it, but we do it because Mom says it's good for us. *Liturgy?* Let's not even go there.

"What time did church start on Sunday morning?" Peter asked.

I found the question kind of odd, since we'd gone together. I shrugged. "Around eight o'clock."

"Wrong. Church started the moment you got in the car. Father Alexander Schmemann is an Orthodox scholar who wrote a book called *For the Life of the World*. He says the liturgy is a journey that proceeds from the kingdom of this world into a brief encounter with the kingdom of God, and then back out again to bear witness to it. The liturgy began the moment you started separating yourself from this world so you could join the rest of the body of Christ. In the liturgy, every act is a metaphor or symbol.

"The word *liturgy* literally means 'work of the people.' It's an ancient text that helps us reenact the redemption drama. What we're reciting is a compressed version of the redemption story. At the end of it, we can't help but be moved to cry out with all the angels and archangels, 'Thanks be to God!' and give our lives to the God who gave his life for us.

"So—you entered sacred space, heard and spoke the Great Story. Next, you were mystically confronted with Christ at the climax of the liturgy—the Eucharist."

I'd heard Catholics and Episcopalians refer to the Lord's Supper as the Eucharist before, but I was unsure what the word actually meant. It's not as if the conservative Baptist seminary I attended emphasized liturgics. I think Peter sensed my uncertainty.

"The word *Eucharist* means 'thanksgiving.' It's that moment in the 'work of the people' when we partake of the divine life and experience the presence of Christ in a way that can be particularly intense," he said.

"I couldn't go up to take it," I said quietly.

"Jesus draws very near at the Eucharist, and that can be unnerving. But think of it as a homecoming celebration. In the Eucharist, we're united with God, all the saints, the earth that gave us the bread and wine, and the whole universe!"

I was silent for a moment, trying to apply what Peter was saying to what had happened to me at Mass. I was coming up empty.

"Perhaps you had trouble believing you were invited to the party," he suggested.

I could feel my face reddening. "Let's move on to you," I said. "What happened? You ended up on the floor."

He smiled. "The Eucharist is the sacrament of love and joy. Sometimes God meets me in it in a way I can't explain."

"You know, Peter," I said, "I'm half-afraid that when this pilgrimage is over I might go home a Catholic."

Standing and stretching, Peter said, "Chase, the pilgrimage is never over."

Journal Entry:
The Friary Solarium

Dear Francis,

I like Catholics, especially Italian ones. If someone weeps in church here, it's just business as usual. They cry lighting candles for a sick relative, looking at Jesus suffering on the cross, or touching the feet of a saint captured in marble. If someone started sobbing uncontrollably during a Communion service at Putnam Hill, people would get freaked. In New England, public displays of emotion give people the hives. What if it's catching? Here you can bawl your eyes out or lie prostrate on the floor, and people step over you like you're a piece of furniture. They assume you're doing what normal people do in the presence of God. Not bad theology.

Peter gave me a book about the Eucharist. It's pretty fascinating. The guy who wrote it says we're not just Homo sapiens (knowing people) but Homo eucharistica (Eucharistic people) as well. In other words, we need more than reason or information to nourish our faith; we're built for firsthand experiences of God through things like the Eucharist as well. It's like what Gandhi said: "The world is so hungry for God that God could only come as a piece of bread. We so long for joy that God even risked coming into the world in the form of intoxication, that risky thing called wine."

Some time back, I heard someone say the Bible isn't simply a book that tells us what to do; it's also a story that tells us who we are. Maybe that's why the liturgy moved me last Sunday. It took me on a guided journey in which I was reminded of who I am, where I came from, how things have gotten so out of whack in this world, how God intervened, and how history is going to end. For so long now I've felt dislocated, and the liturgy helped relocate me. I'm not a character in search of an Author; I have a story.

Over the past two years, my spiritual life has been dying a slow death. Things might have been different if every week I'd sat in a community that repeatedly reminded me of who God is and who I am through something like the liturgy. It would have been like someone saying to me, "Don't worry, Chase. Faith might be hard for you to come by right now, but listen to these ancient words we're saying and 'rent' our faith until yours revives." It's no wonder that most of your writings, Francis, are about the importance of worship, liturgy, and the sacramental life. I understand why I didn't go up for Communion, but now part of me regrets it.

The church we went to last Sunday is called the Chiesa Nuova, which means "new church." Is the new church really the old church rediscovered and contextualized?

VII

Art is the grandchild of God.
DANTE, *Inferno, Canto XI*

ON TUESDAY, CARDINAL MENDOZA CALLED FROM MADRID TO say he was coming to Rome the next day and wondered if Kenny had time to hear his confession. Kenny was more than glad to accommodate his old friend. Assisi is a small place, and the frenzied preparations for Calendimaggio were making it feel smaller, to the point of suffocation. When Kenny asked if I wanted to go with him to Rome, I was ecstatic. I was packed and in the car before he was.

Anatole Broyard said, "Rome was a poem pressed into service as a city." He wasn't kidding. I spent three unforgettable days wandering the streets, visiting museums, jogging around Vatican Square, reading Shakespeare's *Julius Caesar* beside the Trevi Fountain, eating slices of *quattro formaggi* pizza on the steps of the Pantheon, and looking at paintings by local artists in the Piazza Navona. I stood in line for hours to see Michelangelo's miracle on the ceiling of the Sistine Chapel. It's hard to believe one man could actually conceive something so beautiful, much less paint it. Gazing up at *The Last Judgment*, I was humbled by a sense of my own creatureliness. My guidebook wasn't exaggerating when it said it was the most beautiful room in the world.

One of my favorite places was Saint John Lateran's Basilica, the "mother church" of Rome. It's one very impressive building. Thirteen enormous statues sit atop it; the central nave is 425 feet long; and the ceiling is an explosion of color and ornamentation.

In 1209, Francis and a small band of friars came here seeking an audience with Pope Innocent III, hoping to receive a papal blessing for their new order. One afternoon I sat inside the church and read the story of their meeting in the "Legend of the Three Companions":

> On hearing this the Pope was greatly amazed, also because, before Francis appeared, he had had a vision that the church of Saint John Lateran was only saved from falling by being upheld on the shoulder of a small, insignificant man. He had awakened depressed and surprised, and, being wise and discreet, he had pondered long on the meaning of the vision. A few days later blessed Francis and the brothers came to him, and, as we have already explained, he learned the reason of their visit; and blessed Francis appealed to him for the confirmation of the rule, which he had written in brief and simple words, taken for the most part from the Gospel texts, and which he and his brothers strove with all their strength to put perfectly into practice. Then, when the Pope looked at Francis and saw him fervent in the love and service of God, in his own mind he compared his vision of the Lateran with that related by Francis and he began to say to himself: "This is surely a holy and religious man by whom the church of God will be supported and upheld." Then he embraced Francis and approved the rule he had written, and gave him permission to preach penance to all; and this permission was extended to all the brothers who had the approval of Francis.

Sitting in the church, I was struck by the simple elegance of Francis's strategy of ministry — simply read the gospel texts and live the life you find on its pages. *What a concept!* I wondered what Francis would say if he were the main speaker at a church growth conference. Would anyone take him seriously?

By the end of each day I was exhausted, not from the long

hours of walking, but from my senses being flooded with beauty and history. My only regret was that I was alone. It's depressing to be in a city filled with as many splendors as Rome is and not be able to share it with anybody. Kenny's schedule was even fuller than he had anticipated. Every morning over breakfast, he would spend half the time apologizing for not being able to hang out with me, and I would spend the other half assuring him it was fine. I was lying, but there was no sense whining about it.

One afternoon, suffering from tourist burnout, I dropped into a large bookstore that sold titles in English and Italian. In the section displaying those enormous coffee-table books that you buy but never actually read, I noticed a very attractive woman skimming through one with a picture of the Estonian composer Arvo Pärt on the cover. I think of myself as an extrovert, but I've never been good at randomly striking up conversations with people, especially women. Still, I was desperate to talk to someone other than a museum guide or a waiter.

"He's a wonderful composer," I said, hoping she spoke English.

She cocked her head and frowned at me. "You know him?" she asked. I think she was more surprised to meet someone who liked Arvo Pärt than she was by my forwardness.

"Yes, he's one of my favorites," I replied, grateful that her accent was American.

She looked suspicious. "What's your favorite piece of his?" she asked.

I flipped through the pages of a book about Salvador Dali and thought for a moment. "*Berliner Messe*," I answered. "Especially the 'Agnus Dei.'"

She stared at me, then walked a few steps down the aisle and picked up a book about Mahler. "I prefer his orchestral works," she said cautiously. "What other composers do you like?"

I followed her. "John Tavener, James MacMillan, Henryk Górecki—"

She quickly turned. "You like MacMillan?"

"Yes," I said, smiling.

"I've performed with him. He's brilliant," she said.

"You've performed with him?"

She laughed. "Yes, I'm a cellist. I performed 'The Confession of Isobel Gowdie' with him last year."

I struggled to find something intelligent to say. Finally, she saved me. "My name is Carla Mellini," she said, offering me her hand.

"I'm Chase Falson."

"What brings you to Rome?" she asked.

"Long story—I'm visiting my uncle. What about you?"

"I'm here for the spring and summer taking a master class with János Starker and playing with the Sibelius Quartet."

We stood like two seventh graders at their first dance, hoping the other would come up with something to say. Neither of us did.

"It was nice to meet you, Chase," she said finally. "I hope your stay in Rome is a pleasant one." She turned and began walking away.

"Would you like to have coffee?" I blurted.

She turned and looked at me curiously. Glancing down at her watch, she said, "I have a little time. There's a small café here in the bookstore."

I took a seat at a table for two while Carla went to the counter and ordered cappuccinos in Italian. I decided she was probably my age, or maybe a few years younger. She wore sage-colored corduroys and a black cashmere sweater over a white T-shirt. Although her clothing was casual, she was elegant. She carried herself with a dignity and self-assuredness you don't see very often. My mother would have liked her instantly, and in this case that was a compliment.

She carefully placed the hot drinks on the table and sat down.

"What part of Boston are you from?" I asked.

"Beacon Hill," she replied. "How did you know?"

"I went to college with a ton of kids from Boston. You have the more refined Boston accent."

"What you mean is that I don't sound like a Southie," she said, chuckling.

Our conversation took on a natural rhythm. It wasn't long, however, before she asked me the inevitable question: "What do you do for a living?"

I wanted to lie and tell her I was an astronaut, a brain surgeon, or maybe a Formula One driver, something less pedestrian than a minister. I resigned myself to being honest.

"I'm the pastor of a church," I said.

"Oh," she said flatly, idly stirring the foam on top of her cappuccino.

"Is something wrong?"

She sat up straight. "Not at all."

"Really?" I asked.

She let out a long breath. "My parents are very religious. It's been a source of tension between us," she said.

"Why is that?" I asked.

"They think professional musicians are worldly."

"Didn't they pay for your lessons?"

"Actually, no. When I was eight, I received a full scholarship to a private school for the performing arts in Boston. My parents were uneasy about it, but the academics were too good to pass up. They didn't think I'd end up becoming a symphony cellist. 'If you want to play music, you should do it in the church,'" she said, lowering the pitch of her voice to sound like her father. I could only imagine how many times she'd heard those words. "When I told them that I'd been invited to play with the Sibelius Quartet and study with Starker, they reacted like I was joining the carnival."

I shook my head. "So where does that leave you with the whole God thing now?" I asked cautiously.

She shrugged. "I think I still believe. I guess I'm not sure." She broke her biscotti in half and dipped it in her cappuccino. "Tell me about you." She was eager to get the spotlight off herself.

She asked so many questions as I told my story that it took me an hour to get through it.

"So what's next?" she asked.

"I'm not sure. I'm beginning to wonder if I went into the ministry for all the wrong reasons."

"Like?" she asked.

"Maybe to atone for something," I mused out loud. "Or maybe just to hack my father off." We both laughed.

"And what about Francis?" she asked.

"He's still a mystery. Just when I think I've got him figured out, I learn something else about him that blows me away." I looked around to see if anyone was listening. "Want to hear something creepy?"

She hesitated. "Sure."

"Sometimes I feel he's walking right next me," I said. "Sometimes I even talk to him."

"That's not so creepy," she said. "Sometimes when I'm practicing, I feel like Casals is sitting next to me."

The quick cup of coffee turned into two and a half hours. If I'd met Carla back in the States, all my "could this be the one?" bells would have gone off. I was puzzled that I didn't feel that way with her now.

"The Turin Philharmonic is performing tonight," she said, "and there's a free lecture afterward. My friend backed out at the last minute. Maybe you'd like to join me?"

I was thrilled. The idea of spending one more night watching Italian TV or reading books about Saint Francis was less than appealing. I reached into my backpack and pulled out an imaginary date book. "Let me see if I'm available. Tomorrow night the pope and I are having drinks, and the night after that I'm going to the movies with Fellini."

She giggled. "He's dead!"

"Ah, that explains why he said he might be late. Yes, of course I'd like to come. Where do I meet you?"

She stood up and gathered her bags. "It's at the Parco della Musica on the Via Flaminia. Let's meet at the entrance at seven tonight."

I stood up. "*Arrivederci,*" I said.

She smiled. My Italian needed work.

✝ ✝ ✝

That evening, as I read the program, I saw why Carla was so excited about attending this performance — the orchestra was playing Elgar's Cello Concerto in E Minor. From the first note to the last, the concert was electrifying. Every so often I would glance at Carla, who, I could tell, was enraptured. Her fingers couldn't stay still. They mimicked every note the cellist played. I was pleasantly surprised to see that one of my favorite pieces, Finzi's Eclogue for Piano and String Orchestra, op. 10, was part of the evening's program as well. The Eclogue is lyrical and haunting; it surfaces all the unfulfilled desires of your life. My father always told me that my disdain for most atonal works was an indication of my lack of musical sophistication. One more thing I didn't get right.

When the final note was played, Carla was the first person to leap to her feet and cry, "Bravo!" When the applause finally subsided, she grabbed both my hands and said, "Wasn't it magnificent?"

The postconcert lecture was held in a small rehearsal space near the main hall.

The speaker was Liam Cudder, a British musicologist from

Cambridge. I was prepared to see a C. S. Lewis type—a portly man wearing an old houndstooth jacket with leather patches on the elbows, trousers wrinkled from top to bottom. Cudder couldn't have been more different. He was elegantly dressed in a double-breasted blue blazer with gold buttons, perfectly tailored gray flannels, and expensive-looking tassel loafers. His accent betrayed an upper-class pedigree, but there was nothing condescending about him; in fact, he was boyish and animated. He spoke for nearly an hour—deconstructing and analyzing the pieces we'd heard, helping us discover the brilliance of Finzi and Elgar.

Toward the end of the lecture, his remarks took a peculiar turn. "I have spoken for what must seem like an eternity to some of you." The audience laughed. "Now I am interested in knowing what you felt during the concert," he said.

There was an awkward silence. Finally one brave soul said, "Joy."

"Grateful," someone else called out.

Cudder listened to a handful of responses, nodding his head after every reply.

"I am always brought to tears when I hear a marvelous performance followed by a standing ovation," he said. "I feel that at the climax of our cheering, we cross a boundary and unwittingly begin applauding some other reality, a performer we know is there but who cannot be seen. We want to thank Beauty itself."

He held his finger up to his lips and paused. "Let me be bold for a moment. Is it possible that during this evening's performance, we unconsciously sensed Someone standing behind the beautiful, Someone who is its source, and we were moved to praise him as well?"

A hush fell over the room. The good doctor had moved from musicology to theology.

"I am a musicologist, but I am also an ordained priest in the Church of England. For years, I have tried to separate the different hats I wear, but I have been quite unsuccessful; so if you will indulge me, I would like to conclude my remarks this evening by suggesting there is a distinct relationship between beauty and the heart's search for God."

Cudder leafed through his notes. He found the page he was looking for.

"In *Doctor Zhivago*, Boris Pasternak describes one of his main characters like this: 'Lara was not religious. She did not believe in ritual. But sometimes, to be able to bear life, she needed the accompaniment of an inner music. She could not always compose such a music for herself. That music was God's word of life, and it was to weep over it that she went to church.' What was it about music that awakened the spiritual in Pasternak's Lara? It was this: the object of all great art is beauty, and it makes us nostalgic for God. Whether we consider ourselves people of faith or not, art arouses in us what the pope calls a 'universal desire for redemption.'"

Cudder sat on a three-legged stool. "All of us are meaning-seekers. We approach every painting, novel, film, symphony, or ballet unconsciously hoping it will move us one step further on the journey toward answering the question 'Why am I here?' People living in the postmodern world, however, are faced with an excruciating dilemma. Their hearts long to find ultimate meaning, while at the same time their critical minds do not believe it exists. We are homesick, but have no home. So we turn to the arts and aesthetics to satisfy our thirst for the Absolute. But if we want to find our true meaning in life, our search cannot end there. Art or beauty is not the destination; it is a signpost pointing toward our desired destination."

Cudder picked up a page from his notes. "C. S. Lewis puts it so elegantly in *The Weight of Glory*: 'The books or the music in which we thought the beauty was located will betray us if we trust to them; it was not *in* them, it only came *through* them, and what came through them was longing ... For they are not the thing itself; they are only the scent of a flower we have not found, the echo of a tune we have not heard, news from a country we have never yet visited.'" Cudder wisely paused to allow Lewis's words to rest on us. "My hope is that through our future encounters with music and the arts, we will discover this 'heavenly country' we have not yet visited but long to find. Thank you for your very kind attention this evening."

People remained glued to their seats. Cudder's remarks had been spoken with such humility and respect that everyone was charmed. After a few moments, the spell's effect passed, and people gathered their belongings and began leaving.

Carla stood up. "Let's say hello," she said.

Cudder was surrounded by a group of admirers peppering him with questions. Carla and I stood behind them, patiently waiting our turn. Every so often, Cudder would peer over at us curiously, then continue fielding questions. A heavyset woman in red evening wear, dripping pearls and diamonds, asked in a loud, affected voice, "Professor Cudder, what is the true vocation of the artist?" Her question would have been a good one if she hadn't sounded so pleased with herself.

"Perhaps you should ask our friend here," Cudder said, nodding at Carla.

The group turned to look at us.

"If I'm not mistaken, this is Carla Mellini," Cudder said, "one of Europe's most important up-and-coming cellists."

Carla smiled and said, "Thank you, I'm honored."

I looked at Carla out of the corner of my eye. I felt like we needed to be reintroduced.

"Any thoughts, Miss Mellini?" Cudder asked.

Carla took a lengthy pause before answering. "My teacher once told me that artists help people to see or hear beyond the immediate to the eternal. Most people only look at surfaces. A great poem, story, song, or sculpture reveals the hidden meaning of things."

Cudder looked impressed. "But blessed are your eyes because they see, and your ears because they hear," he added, quoting Jesus from the gospel of Matthew.

Everyone in the circle nodded appreciatively. Carla's answer rang true.

"I am sorry to say it is time for us to leave," Cudder announced. "It has been a wonderful evening, but it is getting late and the custodial staff needs to close up. Thank you so much for coming."

As the small band of devotees began filing out, Cudder came to us. "I hope I did not put you on the spot," he said.

"Not at all. And please call me Carla. This is my friend, Chase Falson."

Cudder shook my hand. "Very glad to meet you," he said to us. "My name's Liam. The title Professor is reserved for my students' use." He turned to Carla. "I heard you perform Schumann's Cello Concerto in London last year. It was very stirring."

"It's an amazing piece. I'm glad you enjoyed it," Carla replied.

"Did you enjoy the performance this evening?" Liam asked.

Carla paused. "The orchestra's first cellist is a friend, and he's a wonderful soloist. I wish the slow movement had been more romantic, but otherwise he played it flawlessly."

Cudder began stuffing his notes into a well-worn leather portfolio. "Do you suppose the two of you would join me for a late dinner? I am absolutely famished."

Carla looked at me. "I'm game," I said.

"The Caffe Greco?" Liam suggested.

Carla hesitated. "It's a little pricey," she said. I think she was worried more about the minister's budget than anything else.

"It's my treat," Liam replied.

✝ ✝ ✝

Expensive restaurants in Rome are generally not as opulent as those in Manhattan. Italians care more about great food and creating an intimate atmosphere. The Greco is an exception. Renowned for having been the haunt of famous nineteenth-century writers and artists, it gives you the best of everything—elegant decor, magnificent cuisine, and small tables for easy conversation.

It was yet another feast of food, wine, and passionately expressed ideas. Liam was a true Renaissance man. He was brilliant, funny, and passionate. His rakish good looks and refined demeanor reminded me of a young Roger Moore. We could have listened to him all night.

"The church has a mottled history with artists. In some eras, they have been appreciated, and in others, vilified. There have been seasons when a stifling artistic Puritanism reigned, and others when the arts were celebrated. Some Christians are still ambivalent about art." Liam leaned across the table and spoke as if he were telling us a ghost story around a campfire. "They might arouse the lower passions."

Carla covered her mouth and laughed. Liam flagged down one of the waiters and pointed to our empty champagne bottle. The waiter nodded and ran to the cellar to get us another.

"I came to faith in a Baptist tradition that was suspicious of anything having to do with the imagination," he continued. "They thought it was the source of all kinds of evil ideas and impulses. And, to some degree, that is true. The depraved imagination has the capacity to dream up all sorts of dreadful things, but we threw the baby out with the bathwater. We did not recognize that the redeemed imagination was capable of producing works of beauty that revealed the Glory."

Carla winced. "My parents think the arts are trivial. They say you should go to church to get good teaching, not a sonata," Carla said.

Cudder politely wiped his mouth. "That is ironic, really. First, the Bible is a great literary work of art filled with poetry, songs, stories, parables, history, apocalyptic drama, and wisdom literature. Second, the very people who pride themselves on being focused on the Word often come perilously close to practicing a form of Gnosticism that overvalues the spiritual and eschews the material. But the Word became flesh! The Incarnation proves that the divine can be communicated through the material—color, sound, texture, words printed on paper, the movement of the body."

"Could you write all this down? I'd like to send it to my parents," Carla said.

Liam patted her hand. "Give it time. Your parents will come around. In the meantime, never forget that your vocation is a sacred one."

Carla's face opened up. She looked more relaxed than I'd seen her. She'd met two people in the same day who understood her plight. I could tell that something important was happening for her.

Her expression became pensive. "So maybe I should go back to church?" she asked.

"Now would be the time," he replied.

"Why now?" I asked.

"The church is realizing there is an awareness of God sleeping in the basement of the postmodern imagination and they have to awaken it. The arts can do this. All beauty is subversive; it flies under the radar of people's critical filters and points them to God. As a friend of mine says, 'When the front door of the intellect is shut, the back door of the imagination is open.' Our neglect of the power of beauty and the arts helps explain why so many people have lost interest in church. Our coming back to the arts will help renew that interest."

Carla was spellbound. I tried to imagine what she was thinking. Liam was confirming something she'd probably known all along: her parents were wrong. It was a moment of exoneration.

A lightbulb seemed to go off in Carla's head. "It's like speaking in tongues," she said.

Liam's fork froze halfway between his plate and his mouth. "I'm sorry?" he asked.

Carla sat up straight. "Art, music, dance, theater, literature, film—they're all a way of speaking in tongues!"

"Of course!" I said. "They're spiritual languages that communicate truths about God that human language doesn't have words to express. That's why the church needs to rediscover them."

"What a brilliant way to put it," Cudder said.

"Wait till I tell my Pentecostal parents that I've taken to speaking in tongues. They've been waiting for that to happen for years."

"Wait till they find out you're doing it through your cello," Liam said.

I lifted my glass. "To Beauty!" I said.

Liam and Carla replied, "To Beauty!"

✝ ✝ ✝

"It sounds like the two of you had quite a night," Kenny remarked.

Carla had come to join us for coffee on the veranda overlooking the gardens of our hotel—the Residenza Madri Pie.

The rows of red and white geraniums seemed on the verge of gushing beyond the boundaries of their beds. When I'd first introduced Carla to Uncle Kenny, she'd been reserved, as if wondering whether a friar's way of life isn't a symptom of some delusional pathology. She soon figured out he was exceptional, not psychotic.

Carla looked at me. "I'm not sure which was better, the performance or our time with Liam," she replied.

After dinner, I'd invited Liam to join us for coffee with Kenny as well, but he had to catch an early-morning flight back to England. Saying good-bye wasn't easy. Our conversation might have lasted all night if the owner of the Greco hadn't had to close up.

The three of us swapped e-mail addresses and cell numbers and promised to stay in touch. I hoped it was the beginning of a long friendship.

Kenny flicked the ashes of his cigarette into the ashtray. "Did you say anything about Francis to Liam?" he asked.

"In passing," I said.

Waiting outside the café for a cab, I'd mentioned my interest in Saint Francis, and Liam's face had lit up. He'd clasped me on the shoulder. "Good heavens, man, Francis was an artist par excellence. We'll have plenty to discuss the next time we meet."

"Liam said Francis was an artist," Carla said.

Kenny pushed his chair back and crossed his legs. "A poet, a singer, an actor—some even say a painter. I think that's why so many artists joined the Franciscan Order over the years."

"Like who?" I asked.

"Dante, da Vinci, Cervantes, Giotto, Raphael, Michelangelo, Palestrina, Franz Liszt, and Charles Gounod were all secular Franciscans." Kenny glanced up at Carla, who looked impressed. "Do you know much about the troubadours?" he continued.

"I've heard of them, but that's all," she replied.

"The troubadours were poets and minstrels in the Middle Ages who wrote poems and sang songs about chivalry and courtly love. Francis no doubt met some as he traveled with his father to buy cloth in France. Francis took what he learned from the troubadours and used it in his ministry. Sometimes he'd pick up a stick and put it over his arm, use another as a bow, and play them like a viola, singing and dancing the gospel for hundreds of people at a time. He called his friars the *Jongleurs de Dieu*."

"The *what*?" I asked. "That sounds French. I thought he was Italian."

"It means the 'jugglers of God.' Jongleurs were street jugglers and comedians. Francis wanted his friars to see themselves not only as troubadours but also as wandering jesters proclaiming the gospel. This is why the early Franciscans used songs, storytelling, impromptu dramas, and poetry in their preaching rather than philosophy, logic, or theology," he said.

"Liam said he thought the arts were making a comeback in the church," Carla said.

"I'd like to think so," Kenny said. "For a long time, seminaries have done a good job of producing scholar-pastors. Reason and knowledge have been prized over intuition and imagination. I think we may begin seeing another kind of pastor in postmodernity—the artist-pastor."

"What are they going to wear—smocks and berets?" I asked. Carla and Kenny laughed.

"Hardly," Kenny said. "They'll present the gospel more like Francis did, appealing to both the mind and the mind's eye. When I was in seminary, we studied Aquinas and the Scholastics, who were brilliant at systematizing God. I loved their certainty. Now I think it's the artistic mind, not the scientific mind, that best captures the true nature of God."

Kenny closed his eyes and spoke reverently:

> After the seas are all cross'd, (as they seem already cross'd,)
> After the great captains and engineers have accomplish'd
>   their work,
> After the noble inventors, after the scientists, the chemist,
>   the geologist, ethnologist,
> Finally shall come the Poet worthy that name,
> The true Son of God shall come singing his songs.

"Who said that?" Carla whispered.

"It's from a poem by Walt Whitman—*Leaves of Grass*," Kenny replied.

"It's beautiful," she said.

"But what about people who aren't artists?" I asked, feeling a little left out.

"Francis would say your life should become a poem, a living work of art," Kenny said. "The gift artists bring to the church may be no greater than anyone else's"—he looked directly at Carla—"but we need them desperately."

He'd hit the nail on the head. Tears brimmed in Carla's eyes. Why wasn't I interested in pursuing this woman? She was perfect.

"The Calendimaggio begins tomorrow. Come join us for a few days," Kenny said.

"That would be fantastic," I said.

Carla looked crestfallen. "I'm afraid I can't. The quartet begins rehearsals this afternoon for our next series of concerts. We're performing Beethoven at the Academy of Santa Cecilia," she answered.

I was disappointed. Our friendship was just beginning; there was so much more to talk about. Would this be the last time we would ever see each other?

Kenny stood. "Carla, it's been wonderful to meet you, but I have one last meeting with the Cardinal before we head back to Assisi," he said, shaking her hand. "And you—" he pointed at me like a schoolmaster and smiled—"be ready to leave at five tonight."

"Yes sir," I saluted.

Carla and I sat quietly then. The only sounds were the breeze gently caressing the line of cypress trees surrounding the gardens and the trickling of water from a nearby fountain.

Carla placed her hand on mine. "Chase, the last twenty-four hours have been really important for me. God spoke to me through you and Liam."

"And what did you hear?"

"God said he'd like for us to be friends again."

"Maybe when you go home for a visit, I can drive up to Boston and see you," I said.

"Yes, please. I'll be home at Christmas."

I walked Carla out to the street and waited with her until her bus came. Boarding the bus, she turned and said, "To Beauty."

"To Beauty," I replied. And the doors to the bus closed.

+++

I walked back to the hotel and sat on the veranda. I pulled out my journal and my laptop. I had discovered the night before that the hotel had wireless Internet access. I looked up some of the materials Liam had mentioned the night before.

Journal Entry: The Veranda at the Residenza Madri Pie, Rome

Dear Francis,

A few years ago I went to a U2 concert at Madison Square Garden in New York City, just three months after 9/11. Most of us in the arena that night probably knew someone who'd died in the Twin Towers; we'd lost three people in our church alone. I'll never forget the end of the concert. As the band played the song "Walk On," the names of all those who had died were projected onto the arena walls and slowly scrolled up over us, and then up toward the ceiling. At that moment the presence of God descended on that room in a way I will never forget. There we were, 25,000 people standing, weeping, and singing with the band. It suddenly became a worship service; we were pushing against the darkness together. I walked out dazed, asking myself, "What on earth just happened?" Of course it was the music. For a brief moment, the veil between this world and the world to come had been made thin by melody and lyric. If only for a brief few minutes, we were all believers.

I just looked up John Paul II's Letter to Artists, which Liam had mentioned in his lecture. Here's a part you'd agree with:

"In order to communicate the message entrusted to her by Christ, the church needs art. Art must make perceptible, and as far as possible attractive, the world of the spirit, of the invisible, of God. It must therefore translate into meaningful terms that which is in itself ineffable.

Art has a unique capacity to take one or other facet of the message and translate it into colours, shapes and sounds which nourish the intuition of those who look or listen. It does so without emptying the message itself of its transcendent value and its aura of mystery . . .

"In Christ, God has reconciled the world to himself. All believers are called to bear witness to this; but it is up to you, men and women who have given your lives to art, to declare with all the wealth of your ingenuity that in Christ the world is redeemed: the human person is redeemed, the human body is redeemed, and the whole creation which, according to Saint Paul, 'awaits impatiently the revelation of the children of God,' is redeemed . . . This is your task. Humanity in every age, and even today, looks to works of art to shed light upon its path and its destiny . . .

"Beauty is a key to the mystery and a call to transcendence. It is an invitation to savour life and to dream of the future . . .

"Artists of the world, may your many different paths all lead to that infinite Ocean of beauty where wonder becomes awe, exhilaration, unspeakable joy."

When I became a Christian, I was told that praying to anyone other than God was wrong. But just in case you can hear me, maybe you could offer up a prayer for Carla. It would be wonderful if she rediscovered her faith. My hope is that one day she'll be playing her cello and feel not only Casals next to her, but God as well. Talk to him about that, OK?

✝ ✝ ✝

Rush-hour traffic in Rome makes the Long Island Expressway back home look like a wide-open country lane. By the time we arrived back in Assisi it was ten o'clock. Luckily the trains run almost twenty-four hours. In spite of the late hour, the town was jittery with excitement. The official start of Calendimaggio was the next morning, and workers were still hanging lights and testing sound systems on the open-air stages.

Getting to the friary wasn't easy. Medieval city planners hadn't anticipated the advent of automobiles, and the cobbled streets of Assisi are so narrow and winding that it takes only two or three meandering tourists to snarl up traffic. Kenny and I ended up stuck behind a group of German tourists tottering arm in arm down the Via Portica singing beer-hall songs. German tourists are easy to spot. They come in two varieties. The first are like sleek, expensive BMWs. They're svelte, have perfectly chiseled Aryan features, wear razor-creased blue jeans, and sport those cool, thin, square eyeglasses with titanium frames. They don't smile a lot. The other variety is more like a Volkswagen Beetle. They're the "oompah-pah" types—frumpily dressed, good-natured, and constantly on the prowl for someone to slap on the back. Unfortunately, we got stuck behind a large group of the Volkswagen variety.

"So, tell me more about Carla," Kenny said.

I stared out the passenger-side window. "She's great," I said.

"That's it?"

I sighed. "She puzzles me."

"Why?"

Kenny managed to squeak by the tourists. I thought his side mirror was going to bump one on the butt.

"She's perfect. She's funny, attractive, talented—"

"Available," Kenny added.

I nodded. "All of the above. So why didn't I pursue her? I've never connected with anyone as fast as I connected with Carla, but my heart said don't mess it up by trying to turn it romantic."

"What do you think your heart knew?" Kenny asked.

"I don't know."

A light drizzle began to fall. Kenny turned on the windshield wipers. "Have you read about Francis and Saint Clare?"

"Not much, really," I answered. Every book I'd read about Francis had a chapter about his relationship with Clare. I'd skipped over most of that—I wasn't sure I could handle more than one saint at a time.

"Clare was a young aristocrat who ran away from home to follow Francis. He helped her found an order of nuns who would follow his way of life. Their relationship was very unusual."

"How so?"

"Women in Francis's time were seen as inferior to men. Folks believed they were a dangerous source of temptation to men. Back then, some monasteries wouldn't even allow female animals inside their walls! Francis didn't buy it. He saw that women could have incredible ministries, and he treated them more like equals than most men did in those days. This was pretty revolutionary stuff for the Middle Ages.

"The two of them had a profound love for each other, but it never crossed the border into being romantic. It was more mystical and sublime. They were soul mates who wanted to help each other grow in their common love for Jesus; their relationship was less important than their calling. Franciscan historians say Clare was Francis's dearest friend," he said.

I thought that through, but couldn't see where Kenny was heading. "OK—but what does that have to do with Carla?"

Kenny chuckled. "Maybe nothing. It's just that Francis and Clare modeled a different kind of male-female relationship—one not based on sexual attraction, one that emphasized instead spiritual growth in each of them. Who knows?—maybe that's the kind of relationship God is calling you into with Carla."

I'd only known Carla for two days; all I knew was that I felt oddly warmed toward her, yet not in a romantic sense. I looked out at the passing town and shook my head. "One never knows where a pilgrimage is going to take them," I sighed.

Fed up with a second pack of tourists, Kenny honked his horn and zipped around them. "True enough," he said.

VIII

No one is to be called an enemy,
all are your benefactors, and no one does you harm.
You have no enemy except yourselves.

SAINT FRANCIS OF ASSISI

WHILE WE WERE IN ROME, I HADN'T REALIZED HOW MUCH I WAS missing Thomas, Bernard, and Peter. Though we had only been away for a few days, it was like homecoming week when Kenny and I came down for breakfast the next morning. Bernard greeted us in the refectory like a chubby yellow Lab whose beloved master has just returned from a long trip. His tail wagged so hard I thought his back end would fly off. Peter and Thomas's greetings were more subdued, thank goodness, but just as heartfelt.

After saying grace, Peter poured granola into his cereal bowl. "Tell us all about Rome," he said.

I recounted all the sites I'd visited. Everyone had an opinion about them. Peter and Bernard launched into a heated debate about which church was more beautiful—Saint John Lateran's or Saint Peter's. Even Thomas jumped into the fray, extolling the merits of Santa Maria della Concezione, a weird choice at best. In that one, the remains of four thousand Capuchin friars are buried inside in a crypt filled with soil brought from Jerusalem. A bunch of other friars didn't make it into the crypt, so their skeletons were used to make decorative chandeliers and wall hangings. Even Martha Stewart couldn't have dreamt up this stuff. Soon all three of them were arguing back and forth in Italian and English. It was good to be back.

For three days, Thomas, Peter, Kenny, and I roamed the city together, immersed in the drama of Calendimaggio. Every street played host to a new surprise. We listened to groups of handsome young minstrels dressed in medieval garb, singing courtly love songs to blushing young girls on balconies. We watched crossbow, archery, and banner-hurling contests. We cheered for groups of women performing ring dances in the piazzas and for medieval dramas performed in the streets. The town was a palette of every imaginable color, not to mention good-hearted rowdiness. On the last night, we joined the mob of people packed in front of the Temple of Minerva to find out who had taken the grand prize. The Piazza del Comune was aglow with flaming torches; people were leaning out of windows waving flags; and pale blue and white spotlights illuminated the facade of the temple. Finally the Master of the Field took to the stage to announce the year's winner of the *Palio*, a large red and blue banner with the symbol of the town of Assisi emblazoned on it. The throng held their breath waiting for the results, and the applause was thunderous when the Magnifica Parte de Sotto was declared the victor. Fireworks exploded above our heads, and the people broke out in song. It had been seventy-two hours of pure magic.

The next day, I paid for the excesses of the night before. I didn't awaken until ten o'clock, bleary-eyed and desperate for coffee. I lay in bed for a half hour, trying to convince myself that going to the Internet café to check my e-mail was the right thing to do. I wasn't looking forward to it. Maggie had been keeping me up-to-date on the latest developments at Putnam Hill, and in her last e-mail she'd said the feuding at church had gotten even worse since we last spoke on the phone. Someone was feeding the rumor mill. Had I slept with a member of the church? Did I have a drug problem? Did I watch SpongeBob? People were accusing the leadership of withholding information, and two of the elders had already resigned and left the church—another was on the fence, but it looked like he might leave as well. Maggie said Chip wasn't doing much to muzzle the gossips. To the contrary, she thought it likely he was starting some of it himself. I was tempted to pick up the phone and call a few friends to find out what was actually going on, but the elders were adamant about my not talking to people in the congregation. Maggie was an exception, I felt.

I dragged myself out of bed, grabbed a cup of coffee from the refectory, and headed over to the café. I opened my e-mail and saw one from Ed. It took me several minutes to muster the courage to open it.

> *Chase,*
>
> *It's been several weeks since you left, and the elders want to know when you plan to return. Things have been difficult since your departure, but we're hanging in there and praying for the Lord's guidance. We trust you are as well.*
>
> *On a more personal note, I want to apologize for what I said to you at the door of your condo. I realize now that I spoke out of anger and not out of love. Regardless of how this all plays out, I'll always consider you my brother in Christ and my friend as well.*
>
> *Let me know your thoughts ASAP.*
>
> *Ed*

I read and reread Ed's e-mail, enjoying the rush of gratitude coursing through my heart. Ed wasn't a vulnerable man. I knew what it had cost him to write those words. His apology lifted an onerous burden off my shoulders that I'd been carrying around for weeks.

Even so, I did not want to commit to a date to go home to face the elders. I had done a lot of thinking about the future, and I was still confused. I wasn't sure yet whether I should resign or ask the church to forgive me and give me a second chance. I felt as if my new friendship with Francis was birthing something important in me. I was holding the church and my faith up to the light, like a prism—and I was discovering new colors in them. And yet my gut told me the pilgrimage wasn't finished. I still had more to learn. I tried to compose a reply to Ed, but the words just wouldn't come. I decided to wait a day or two.

As I was logging off, I looked up through the café window—and there was Bernard, jumping up and down and waving. He had been strangely absent during Calendimaggio. Every morning, he'd gotten up early to make the sixteen-mile drive to Perugia for meetings. Thomas had said he was working on a special project, and I hadn't probed further. Now, standing next to him was an extraordinary-looking black woman, smiling serenely and wearing the habit of a Franciscan nun. I couldn't hear Bernard's words, but I could read his lips: "Come outside, I want you to meet someone."

✛ ✛ ✛

"Sister Irene is a senior fellow at the Franciscan Peace and Reconciliation Institute in Rome. We met eight years ago at a conference in Palestine," Bernard explained as we sauntered down the Via del Seminario. After we'd been introduced on the steps of the café, Sister Irene had asked if we could visit her favorite *gelateria* in Assisi. Gelato is what heaven would taste like if someone froze it and crammed it into a paper cup. It's made with whole milk, eggs, sugar, and fresh seasonal fruits, all whipped together and refrigerated until it takes on a silky-smooth texture. Italians are dead serious about their gelato. Families jealously guard their recipes like dragons guard their gold. Every so often, an American tourist makes the ill-fated mistake of walking into a gelateria and ordering "ice cream." They usually find his body two days later, bobbing in the Tiber.

Sister Irene linked arms with Bernard, "Yes, the conference in Palestine was wonderful, and we became good, good friends," she said. The pitch of Irene's voice modulated up and down, the word *good* sounding like a breathy train whistle.

"What was the conference about?" I asked.

"International conflict resolution," Bernard replied.

"Jimmy Carter spoke," Sister Irene added. "He was remarkable." Her accent was enchanting and lyrical.

"Where are you from?" I asked.

"I am from Rwanda," she said. My heart skipped a beat. After seeing the movie *Hotel Rwanda*, I'd walked out of the theater and driven straight to Borders to buy books about the 1994 genocide that swept across that small nation in Central Africa. In just ninety days, the Hutu-dominated government and militia—the Interahamwe—had killed nearly one million Rwandan Tutsis and moderate Hutus. The killing was unspeakably horrible; most of the victims were butchered with machetes and clubs.

Bernard wrapped an arm around his friend's shoulder.

"I have seen more than my share of war," she continued. "In the seventies, I was in Beirut. During the early nineties I was in Sarajevo, and right after the genocide my superiors sent me home to Rwanda to launch a peace and reconciliation program."

I shook my head. "What a journey," I said.

She looked at me and grinned. "Yes, but we go where the Lord calls us, do we not?"

"Yes, I suppose we do," I said, looking sideways at her, wondering what Bernard had told her about me.

We sat on a bench outside the main entrance to the Basilica di San Francesco for an hour, talking about Rwanda and how terrible conditions were across Africa. Touch was Irene's second language. As she spoke, she would affectionately place her hand on my shoulder, knee, or arm.

"Tomorrow," she said, "I am traveling to a conference in Perugia on peacemaking. Perhaps you would come as an observer?"

"It's for high school and college students," Bernard added.

"Are you going?" I asked him.

Sister Irene laughed. "Is he going? He is chairing it!"

Now I understood where he had been the past few days.

After several weeks in Italy, I was learning to go wherever the Spirit led. Openness to the movement of God was vital to the pilgrim life. I smiled and shrugged. "Sure, I'll come," I said.

✝ ✝ ✝

Somewhere along the circuitous path of history, Catholics had lost their architectural minds. The conference was held in a large, unimaginatively constructed retreat center built in the 1950s. A few days earlier, I'd been confused when Peter complained that the aesthetic sensibilities of Catholics had never recovered from the invention of folk guitars and cinder blocks. Now I got it.

But my disappointment in the conference center's appearance evaporated the moment Irene and I stepped inside. Hundreds of young people from all over the world were there. Wandering around the registration area I spotted name tags from Iraq, Northern Ireland, Sudan, Mozambique, Burundi, Congo, England, the United States, Indonesia, and Nicaragua. All were dressed in the traditional garb of their native countries. The room was aflame with colorful attire and buzzing with energy. Some of the students had come from universities where they were majoring in peace and reconciliation studies; others were aspiring peace activists who were interning in parts of the world I wouldn't dare set foot in. This wasn't a love-in for glassy-eyed peaceniks; these kids were all business.

As the convener of the conference, Bernard opened the program. Projected onto a large screen behind him was the famous photograph of the lone man facing down the tank in China's Tiananmen Square. That picture never fails to inspire me; it's my generation's icon of human courage. Bernard stepped up to the microphone, and of course there was the obligatory blast of feedback. We all covered our ears and winced.

"May I ask you to take your seats, please?" he asked, looking embarrassed. After a few moments the crowd settled down.

"My name is Father Bernard Mays, and I wish to welcome you to this year's Institute for Franciscan Peace Studies conference." There was an enthusiastic round of applause. Bernard smiled and held up his hands. "Our planning team has worked very hard to make this year's conference one that will leave a deep impression on our lives and ministries. Our theme is 'A Franciscan Vision for Peace in the New Millennium.' Given the current global situation, I can't think of a more critical or timely topic for Christians than our call to be peacemakers.

"Our first plenary speaker is someone many of you know personally, others only by reputation. Dr. Emmanuel Mukamana is a pediatrician, an ordained deacon in the Catholic Church, and, most important," Bernard said smiling, "the brother of Sister Irene Mukamana, one of our Fellows at the Institute in Rome." I looked at Irene sitting posture-perfect in the chair next to me, hands folded quietly in her lap, her high-set cheekbones giving her an air of royalty and providing cover for her faint smile of pride.

"Along with his sister, Dr. Mukamana oversees a nationwide reconciliation program in Rwanda partially funded by the Institute for Franciscan Peace Studies. In 2002, his work was awarded the Albert Schweitzer Prize for providing the global community with a practical and inspiring model for Christian peacemaking. The world doesn't need abstract discussions about peacemaking and reconciliation; they need to see it brought to life in flesh and blood, and I know of few people who embody the ministry of reconciliation like Emmanuel Mukamana." Bernard began the applause, then gestured, inviting Emmanuel forward. The students applauded and whistled as Emmanuel climbed the stairs onto the stage. The broader he smiled, the louder the applause grew. He looked to be in his mid-forties. Wearing dark jeans and an Oxford University sweatshirt, Mukamana appeared to be a collision of opposites — humility and greatness, playfulness and gravity.

"*Amahoro!*" he cried into the microphone, cupping his ear to encourage us to answer.

"*Amahoro!*" we yelled back.

Emmanuel chuckled. "In my country, *amahoro* means 'peace,' so already we have begun by obeying Francis's command that we greet everyone by saying 'The peace of the Lord.'"

He cleared his throat. "I have come because I have a story. It is not an unfamiliar tale in my native land, but it is mine, and it is all I can offer you. For two years after the genocide, I could not speak of the things I saw. But one night our Lord Jesus told me not to hide my pain under a rock anymore, but to tell it to many so it might earn interest.

"In 1994, my family and I, who are Tutsi, were living in a town called Ruhengeri in Rwanda, near the border of Uganda. I was one of three doctors working in a government-subsidized health clinic, along with my wife, Mercy, who is a nurse practitioner. On April the 29th, I was seeing patients when my wife's best friend, Eugenia, ran into our office holding an infant covered in blood. The baby's mother had run into her yard clutching the baby and screaming that Hutu militia had set up roadblocks on either end of town and were killing Tutsi. The mother had handed the baby to Eugenia and then collapsed. I knew from the child's unresponsive eyes that it was already dead, but I had no time to attend to it," he said. "You see, our eight-year-old twin sons, Nathan and Concord, were at school when the killing started. Mercy and I then tried to get to them on foot, but a truck full of Interahamwe soldiers had parked in the middle of town and were passing out machetes and clubs to other Hutu. People we had

known all our lives, people I had treated as patients, the parents of
our children's friends, suddenly were going from house to house
murdering whole families. Some were paid to do it, some were
forced, and others took little convincing.

"There was no way to get to the school without being caught
by one of the roving bands, so Mercy and I ran to the home of my
secretary and her husband, who are Hutu but our dearest friends
as well. They risked their lives by hiding us in an abandoned well
in their backyard. We lost track of time as we sat and prayed in
that muddy hole, listening to the sound of gunfire and screaming
above us. Late that night, some drunken Hutu sat on the lip of the
well, laughing and smoking, talking of how they'd raped women
before killing them—all while we barely breathed twenty feet
below them.

"After they left, I scaled the side of the well and made my
way to Nathan and Concord's school. I hid in a grove of trees
and watched the building from a distance to make sure there
were no Interahamwe there. It seemed deserted and quiet, but as
I approached I knew something was very wrong. The doors and
windows were smeared in blood. I was so panicked that my heart
was beating like this," Emmanuel said, slapping his chest quickly
with his hand.

"I ran to Nathan and Concord's classroom, and what I saw—"
Emmanuel paused.

I wondered how many times now he had forced himself to tell
this story—and whether it would ever get any easier to tell.

"The children's bodies were piled in a corner of the room like
firewood. The desks had been knocked over as if the children
had been chased around the room as a group. Near the top of
the pile was the body of Concord, his neck nearly severed. I collapsed against the blackboard and vomited. After a few minutes,
I thought I heard raspy breathing, and I froze. What if the killers
were outside? Then I realized that the sound was coming from the

pile of dead children. I began the difficult task of pulling the pile apart until I found my Nathan underneath the body of his brother. He was quivering and trying to speak. Both his arms were broken and badly hacked; he had put them up to shield his body from the blows of the machetes. We think he must have blacked out from terror during the attack, and the Interahamwe mistakenly assumed he was dead," Emmanuel said.

As I listened to Emmanuel, the ache of grief in my chest was so devastating that I could barely breathe. I surveyed the room, and it was clear I wasn't alone. Everywhere I looked, tears were flowing freely.

"Thank God I was able to carry Nathan back to my secretary's home without getting caught. She drove to the clinic to get the supplies I needed to treat Nathan, and we lived in the well for two months until we were able to flee to a refugee camp in Uganda. Later, Nathan told us that the assistant headmaster had led the militia to his classroom and pointed to the children who were Tutsi. He drank beer and watched as my son and his classmates were slaughtered. Six hundred in one afternoon." Emmanuel took a sip of water, then stood silently for a moment before continuing.

"We returned to Ruhengeri in 1995, and I discovered that this assistant headmaster and his family were living in our house. I saw his nine-year-old boy wearing my dead son's clothes and riding his bicycle in the road. Can you imagine such a thing? Many Tutsi came home to discover this had happened to them. When I confronted the man, he denied he had anything to do with the killing and claimed he had a right to be in my home, since we had deserted it. In my rage I tried to kill him, but our neighbors pulled us apart. We went to stay with my sister's family in the next town over. It took me more than a year to have the man and his family evicted. Even though he was eventually arrested and imprisoned, I remained filled with such hatred, such a desire for revenge, that I could not sleep at night. I dreamed of killing not only him but also his whole family, so that he might know the depths of my suffering. But there is an old Rwandan proverb: 'He who seeks vengeance is like a man who drinks poison, hoping that it will kill his enemy,' " Emmanuel said, a fleeting smile appearing for just a moment. "I knew my heart was dying, and I begged the Lord to save me."

He looked in my direction and smiled. It took me a moment to realize he was smiling at Sister Irene, seated next to me.

"Today," he said, "my sister and I run a program to bring together people who participated in the genocide with people whose loved ones were murdered. The families and friends of the victims talk about their grief, while the people who took part in the genocide listen. Afterward, the perpetrators can confess what they did during the genocide and ask forgiveness. My healing came when I came face-to-face with two men who had participated in the massacre at my sons' school. Before a large group, my wife and I described to them what their crimes had done to our hearts, how Nathan has nightmares and wets himself now. As we told our story, one of the men began sobbing. He said he had been forced to take part in the killing, and he begged us to forgive him.

"As he wept, a three-year-old Tutsi girl waddled across the room and climbed up into his lap to comfort him. Her gesture overwhelmed us. We all wailed so long that I thought we would never stop. That was a turning point for me." Emmanuel stopped for a moment, lost in his memories.

"That little girl showed me the gospel, and the power of forgiveness and reconciliation, not to mention what it means to be a peacemaker. She brought Francis's words to life: 'We should love our enemies because their injurious conduct gives us an occasion to gain eternal life by returning love for hatred.' Without forgiveness, there is no peace. *Umwami imanaiguhe amahoro*—the Lord give you peace," he said and walked off the stage.

There was a long pause as people tried to absorb what Emmanuel had shared. But soon everyone in the room was on their feet, applauding and crying. As I joined in, I wondered if it wasn't time for the human family to devise a new way of expressing admiration and thanks, something reserved for those times when mere clapping is absurdly inadequate.

+ + +

Sister Irene had to teach a class. I joined her afterward. We grabbed a box lunch and walked outside. It was sunny and warm, but gusty winds blew down off the mountains, buffeting us as we walked. Irene had to press down her habit to prevent it from blowing up, and I had to hold her by the arm so she wouldn't end up becoming The Flying Nun. We found a rickety wooden bench leaning against a wall at the back of the conference center that provided shelter from the wind.

Irene smoothed the paper bag her lunch came in and used it as a place mat on her lap. "So what do you think so far?" she asked.

"I'm impressed." The class I had attended while Irene taught hers had been about Francis's approach to peacemaking. The instructor, an American friar named Brother Frank who lived and worked among Palestinians, had been delighted with the students' participation—they had challenged and stretched him. "These kids know their business. I was nothing like them when I was their age," I said.

"What were you like?"

I thought for a moment. "My relationship with Jesus was more personal," I replied. "I never thought about how faith related to big global issues."

Irene put down her sandwich. "I've always found the phrase 'personal relationship with Jesus' a little puzzling. I don't mean to be rude, but it sounds so self-interested. I've always had an intimate relationship with Jesus, but my faith is more rooted in the communal than the personal."

I was beginning to see her point. During my time at the friary, I'd experienced Jesus' presence in a way I never had before, and it had come through being in such close community. Eating together, praying together, living together, doing life that closely with a group of Christians was something new to me. The faith I'd embraced was more an individualistic enterprise than anything else. "Can I ask you a personal question?" I said, peeling my orange.

"Of course."

"Emmanuel found peace. What about you?" I asked.

Sister Irene sighed. "Some days I feel like I have forgiven the Interahamwe, and other times I pray the Lord's Prayer and feel like a hypocrite. I begin to think forgiveness is not something you do; it is something that gets done to you."

I cocked my head. "What do you mean?"

"Perhaps the power to forgive cannot be manufactured, but is a *charism* you receive," she said.

"I hope so. I haven't been very successful at generating it on my own."

"You need to make peace with someone?" Irene asked.

I chuckled. "Let me see ... my parents, the church, God, my childhood—"

Irene frowned, grasped my hand, and looked me square in the eye. "Do you really want peace?"

"Yes," I said.

"And you want to spread peace to the world?"

"Yes."

Irene's face softened. "You cannot—until you have peace with yourself," she said, releasing my hand and placing her own over my heart. Warm currents of healing passed through her fingers. The bruises on my heart were exposed. Was this what lepers felt like when Jesus touched them?

She closed her eyes. "While you are proclaiming peace with your lips, be careful to have it even more fully in your heart.

Nobody should ever be roused to wrath or insult on your account. Everyone should rather be moved to peace, goodwill, and mercy because of your restraint. For we have been called to the purpose of healing the wounded, binding up those who are bruised, and reclaiming the erring."

"Who said that?" I whispered.

Irene beamed. "Who do you think? Francis could not be a peacemaker until he had peace about his broken relationship with his father, his lost dreams, his own demons. It is no different for us. If we want to be peacemakers, we have to confront the wounds and darkness in our own hearts first—otherwise we will always be blaming others for our problems instead of looking at ourselves. And you know what, Chase?" She looked me in the eye. "No one else is ever the cause of your problem."

My face went hot. "I don't think you under—"

"Yes, the church needs rebuilding; yes, your parents failed you; yes, you are a broken person; yes, your tradition is not everything you thought it was—but do not blame anybody or anything else for your lack of peace or your problems." She paused and squeezed my hand. "*You* are the biggest problem you have."

My first impulse was to fight back, but my own heart silenced me, saying, *Amen*.

✝ ✝ ✝

Irene and I spoke for so long that we missed the next speaker. Because she had other responsibilities, she asked two students, Jamal and Terence, to be my guides for a few hours. They took me under their wings, introducing me to friends who were more than willing to talk about their peacemaking ministries and programs. The whole day was an aperture-opener, as if someone had plucked me out of the weeds of my narrow, self-concerned faith and shot me up to fifty thousand feet so I could look down at another facet of what it meant to be a follower of Jesus.

Around eleven that night, all the conference attendees boarded buses to head out to the closing ceremonies. "Where are we going?" I asked.

"The Spoleto Valley," Jamal said.

"Why?" I asked.

"You'll see," Terence said.

As we got off the bus, we were given a box of matches, a brown paper bag, and a votive candle. Bernard and a small band of friars were already out in an open field waiting for us. It was difficult to hear him as he yelled instructions over the din of the crowd. "Form a circle!" he cried. There's a reason Jesus called people lost sheep. They're hard to herd. It took Bernard and five other friars about ten minutes to get the group into formation. I fell into place beside Irene. Once we were organized, Bernard began speaking.

"Imagine Francis as a young man dressed for battle. He's riding his horse across these fields to join the army of the great Walter of Brienne. He's convinced that his call is to win glory as a knight, as a man of violence and war. But when Francis reaches Spoleto, he hears Jesus tell him to return home. Jesus has a different plan for his life. In time, Francis realizes that God is not calling him to be a soldier but to preach a gospel of peace and reconciliation. Every year, we end our conference by coming here to recommit our lives to be peacemakers in the world, as Francis was. So let's begin by lighting the candles inside our bags and placing them on the ground in front of us."

Lighting the candles took a while. Luckily, the wind had died down, and the night was calm. The flickering candles inside the bags were eerily beautiful. Their glow shone up and gently illuminated the faces of everyone in the circle.

Bernard continued. "Now I invite you to pray out loud the names of people you know who have lost their lives in conflicts around the world."

The evening's calm was interrupted by a litany of loss. Some spoke plainly, others through sobs. *Seamus. Ivan. Linda. Rafique. Ahmad. Benjamin.* Once upon a time, each of those people had been bearers of dreams and hopes. Some had been children; others, wives or husbands. All had left loved ones behind who now saw their faces only late at night as they passed beneath the silent gate of sleep.

After a few minutes, Bernard had the other leaders give out vials of oil so we could recommission each other as peacemakers. I felt like an impostor. I didn't live in Iraq or Palestine. The only war I'd ever been in was over a parking space at the mall. *Who was I to take part in this ceremony?*

But when the vial of oil reached Irene, she turned to me. Looking into her eyes, my discomfort vanished. Her face was incandescent. She placed a droplet of oil on the tip of her finger and signed my forehead with the cross. "Chase, I anoint you in the name of the Father and the Son and the Holy Spirit. May you have peace—not the peace that the world gives, but the peace of Jesus."

Throughout the commissioning service a song was sung. I'd heard the words to it a million times, and under most circumstances I'd have said the whole thing was corny. But after all I'd learned that day about peace, and about Francis all along, the words of his prayer took on a new depth of meaning.

> Lord, make me an instrument of your peace.
> Where there is hatred, let me sow love;
> where there is injury, pardon;
> where there is doubt, faith;
> where there is despair, hope;
> where there is darkness, light;
> where there is sadness, joy.
> O Divine Master, grant that I may not so much seek
> to be consoled as to console;

to be understood as to understand;
to be loved as to love.
For it is in giving that we receive;
it is in pardoning that we are pardoned;
and it is in dying that we are born to eternal life.

Journal Entry:
The San Rufino Friary

Dear Francis,

*Tonight was one of those rare times when I felt like the curtain
between heaven and earth became very thin. I saw another dimension
of what it meant to be a Christian, and I was (am) grateful.*

*Listening to Brother Frank today, I realized I've confused being
a peace lover with being a peacemaker. A peace lover is someone who
enjoys the absence of conflict, but a peacemaker is someone who is
proactively engaged in works of reconciliation in every sphere of life, from
the personal to the global. That's a whole different spiritual ball game
from the one I've been playing. I've always stayed away from this stuff
because it smelled of "liberal" politics and theology. But is being an
advocate for peace and justice and encouraging leaders to follow a biblical
program for peacemaking an indication of anything except wanting to be
obedient to the gospel? This is a lot to process in one day. It's giving me
a lot to think about.*

*In one of the handouts I got at the conference, there's a quote by
Donald Spoto from his book called* Reluctant Saint. *"When Francis
insisted on the need for peace, it was more than just a sentimental
wish; it was a prayer for the human condition. It derived from his
acquaintanceship with Scripture, from hearing the words spoken at
worship, and from his direct inner experience of the peace of God, which
had changed and was continuing to change his life as his own conversion
continued . . . Francis embarked each day on his mission to proclaim
God's peace to a violent world. Much more than the mere absence of
conflict, peace was to be the result of better relationships with God and
neighbor, and was therefore necessarily linked to justice and love."*

I love what G. K. Chesterton said centuries later about this kind of Christianity: "What a wonderful idea—and a great pity so few have ever tried it!"

Francis, your genius was that you read stuff in the Bible (like the Sermon on the Mount), and you didn't spiritualize or theologize it. You heard Jesus say, "Happy are the peacemakers," so you got up every day and embarked on a new peace mission. My usual approach is to read the Bible, try to understand what it's saying, and then apply it. Your formula was the reverse. You applied the Bible, and then came to a fresh understanding of what it actually meant. What a concept!

Sister Irene really nailed me on some stuff. She was right on a lot of it too. I've done plenty of whining and blaming in my life. You once said, "Above all the grace and the gifts that Christ gives to his beloved is that of overcoming self." My self could use a little overcoming.

Your friend,
Chase

IX

Preach as you go!
SAINT FRANCIS OF ASSISI

THE NEXT MORNING, I WOKE UP LATER THAN USUAL. A BESOTTED dog on a nearby street had barked at the door of his beloved most of the night, making me nearly homicidal. Francis would have gone out and politely asked the dog to be quiet until morning, and the dog would have licked his face and obeyed. I imagined going out and thrashing him with a three iron.

Dragging myself out of bed, I unlatched the wooden shutters on my bedroom window. The morning sun warmed my face as I watched cars snaking their way along the roads that wind through the open valley, amber plumes of dust following in their wake. I was envious knowing that all those people had places to go, and that at day's end they would return home to excited children and leisurely dinners. They were blessed with the certainty of destination. Where would I go when my pilgrimage was over? Francis was teaching me more about what it meant to follow Jesus than I'd learned in a long time, but to what end? How would I apply all this new knowledge? Having spent most of my life ducking existential questions, I felt overwhelmed.

I decided to head back to the San Damiano Chapel to spend some time in solitude. I wanted Jesus to speak to me from the crucifix, just as he had to Francis. *Who knows,* I thought, *maybe he'll say, "Go back to Thackeray, and you will be told what to do. Your new calling will be revealed to you there."* I knew a theophany doesn't happen every day, but hope still runs on fumes.

En route to the chapel, I stopped at the Café Trovelessi for an espresso. First thing in the morning, Italians stop at espresso bars on their way to work for *caffe* and biscotti. Most don't sit down at a table to savor the experience. They lean against the bar and throw back the small puddle of black mud like cowboys slinging shots of whiskey. The caffeine rush is so intense that it requires two people to manage the event—the barista to make the espresso and another to stand by with defibrillator paddles. I grieved the thought of having to go home to American coffee.

On my way out the door, Kenny had given me a copy of Simone Weil's *Waiting for God*. I'd already read a few chapters, and my interest was piqued. Now, sauntering up the Corso Mazzini toward the Porta Nuova, I was looking forward to a quiet morning of reading and journaling. Near the top of the stairs leading down to the San Damiano Chapel, I passed the bus stop where Kenny and I had first arrived in Assisi. The bus from Perugia had just rolled in, and morning commuters were getting off. As I worked my way through the crowd, I heard luggage falling down the bus stairs. "Look out below!" someone screamed.

I froze in my tracks, sure I was having an auditory hallucination. I knew that voice as well as my own. I turned around, and there was Maggie. She'd fallen head over heels down the bus stairs and was sprawled like a Raggedy Ann doll on top of an old duffel. It had been only a few weeks since I'd last seen her, but she looked like she'd been a guest on a complete makeover show. Her auburn hair was now blonde, and she'd managed to squeeze two or three more silver hoops onto each of her earlobes. She stood, brushed off her clothes, and unleashed a string of expletives that would have made a trucker blush.

"Maggie?"

She turned. "Hey!" she screamed, and ran to hug me, then stepped back and grinned. "Surprised?" she asked.

I tried to speak, but all that came out were gargling sounds.

Seeing Jesus on roller skates would have surprised me less. "What on earth are you doing here?" I asked.

She slung her bag over her shoulder. "It's a long story," she said.

✝ ✝ ✝

"She's utterly charming," Peter whispered in my ear.

Maggie and I had trudged back to the friary with her luggage. When we arrived, all the guys were in the refectory lazing around after breakfast. After I'd introduced her to everyone, Maggie sat at the table and explained what had inspired her to come to Assisi.

"I had this dream," she said.

Kenny's eyes widened. "A dream?" Kenny was smitten with Maggie. I'm not sure, but I think there's a weird, instant rapport among smokers.

"I was standing on the observation deck of the Empire State Building," she said, "thinking how I needed to move out of my apartment 'cause it's way too expensive and everything in it reminds me of my daughter." Maggie's voice trailed off. Iris's death was so fresh in her mind that whenever she spoke about it, a dark shadow passed over her eyes and she turned inward, searching for a hidden spring of strength to finish speaking.

"Then I see this short guy standing in front of one of those thingies that you put a quarter in to get a better view of the city," she continued.

"A roof telescope?" Bernard said.

"That's it," she said. She was talking so fast I was having trouble following her myself. "He asks me if I want to take a look. So I put my eyes up to it and see Chase standing in a field. And guess what?"

"What?" Thomas asked.

"Chase is standing in the field next to the same guy who asked me if I wanted to look through the telescope! The guy was in two places at the same time! Then he whispers in my ear, 'Go to Italy.' And when I turn to ask him why, he's gone." Maggie pulled out a neon-yellow lighter with "One Day at a Time" printed on it and fired up another Marlboro Light. "Is that bizarre or what?" she asked, blowing a stream of smoke toward the ceiling.

Thomas smiled and gazed out the window. "Perhaps not," he said.

"The next day, I couldn't get the dream out of my head, so I called my girlfriend Gina," Maggie continued. Gina was Maggie's AA sponsor and the woman who first told Maggie about our church.

Bernard leaned toward her. "And she said?"

"She said, 'Pack your bags, honey! Sounds like God to me.'"

I was still reeling from shock, but I stood and began pacing around the room. "But Maggie, where did you get money for airfare?"

Maggie worked as a hostess at one of the more upscale restaurants in Thackeray and barely made enough to keep her head above water. I once spent an entire night helping her write a budget plan. When we were done, she'd insisted on putting all her maxed-out credit cards in a blender and pureeing them. She had a flair for the dramatic.

"I sold my car to buy the plane ticket," she said blithely.

I grabbed the back of a chair to steady myself. "You what?" I asked.

"And don't worry, I was thinking about getting a different job anyway," she said, dismissing my incredulity with a wave of her hand.

"You walked out of your job?" I said.

"That disgusting bartender at Le Chateau couldn't keep his hands off me," she said, shuddering.

Wires were crossing and shorting in my head. A part of me was thrilled to see Maggie. I'd always had a soft spot in my heart for her. Every day, she had to make the choice between living a life of guilt or one of grace, and usually she got it right. She'd come a long way, but she was still a bruised and tender reed. On the other hand, I felt invaded, like someone had rudely crashed my private party. What on earth was I going to do with her?

Peter stood and stretched. "I, for one, am delighted you're here. You've come on just the right day. We'd planned on taking Chase to Greccio this morning," he said.

That was news to me.

Bernard frowned. "Peter, Maggie might be too tired from her travels," he said.

"Heck, no. I'm willing and able," Maggie said.

Kenny reached to pick up Maggie's bag, but Thomas beat him to it. People were falling over themselves to help her.

"I'll have Sister Raisa make up a room for you in our guest wing," Bernard said.

"Why don't we all meet in front of the chapel in half an hour?" Peter suggested.

Everyone scurried off to their rooms to get ready except me. I sat on the edge of the breakfast table and stared at the smoldering remains of Maggie's cigarette. I was wondering if my pilgrimage had just gone up in smoke.

✝ ✝ ✝

Kenny borrowed the friary's minivan so that all six of us could go to Greccio in one car. On the way, the guys gave Maggie a crash course on the life of the "Beloved Saint." She wasn't nearly as skeptical about Francis as I had been at first; she hung on their every word.

When they finished, Maggie elbowed me. "This Francis guy was very cool," she said.

Everyone burst out laughing. More books have been written

about Francis than about almost any other mortal in history, and she managed to reduce his life to one pithy adjective—*cool*.

Maggie fumbled around in her big, pink vinyl handbag, looking for a piece of gum. It sounded like a plumber rummaging through his toolbox. "Those are great stories," she said, "but I still don't get it. What was his point?"

Bernard looked at Maggie in the rearview mirror. His brows were furrowed. "What do you mean?"

Maggie took the wrapping off a tired-looking piece of Bubble Yum Mega Cherry and popped it into her mouth.

"Putnam Hill has a mission statement. What was Francis's?" she asked.

I was amazed by the laser focus of Maggie's question. I had done all this reading about Francis, but it had never occurred to me to ask the guys for a clear précis of his mission. I was as interested in their answer as Maggie was.

Kenny was the first to speak up. "The Rule of 1221 said that Franciscans were to 'proclaim the Word of God openly, calling on people to repent, believe, and be baptized.'"

Maggie screwed up her face and looked out her window. Lines of olive trees, light-pink houses with moss-covered roofs, and the occasional old man on a rickety bicycle dotted the landscape. She blew an enormous bubble and popped it. "Big deal. Aren't we all supposed to do that?"

Maggie was the most straightforward person I'd ever known. Six months in the slammer has a way of teaching you how to cut to the chase.

"True," Thomas said. "But it's the way Francis preached and evangelized people that made him special."

Kenny parked on a thin stretch of grass on the side of the road. A short distance away, we could see the hermitage on top of Mount Lacerone. As we trekked toward it, Bernard gave us a little more background. "Francis first came to Greccio in 1217, and his preaching was so powerful that almost the whole town was converted and joined his order on the spot. One of the new believers was a wealthy man named Giovanni di Velita. He decided that keeping Francis around would be good for the community, so he offered to build him a hermitage."

Bernard was huffing and puffing from walking up the steep incline. Peter picked up the story. "At first, Francis said no, worried that the brothers would be too distracted from their life of prayer if they lived in the village. Giovanni was persistent, and Francis finally gave in. His only condition was that the hermitage be built at least a stone's throw away from the town. So one night he asked a boy to throw a lit torch and said that wherever it landed would become the site of their new retreat."

Maggie giggled. "That's crazy," she said.

"Stick around," I whispered.

Thomas pointed at the hermitage. "The torch flew over a mile away—to here," Thomas said.

"The kid must have had quite an arm," Maggie said.

Kenny laughed and put his arm around her shoulders. "Yes, I suppose he did."

✝ ✝ ✝

Greccio blew Maggie away. It was impossible to keep up with her. She was a hummingbird, flitting from one fresco and cave to another. Soon she discovered the dormitory where Francis and the friars slept.

"Whoa, I thought my apartment was small. How did all those guys fit in here?" she asked, looking around.

Thomas took her by the hand. "Come over here," he said gently. He pointed to a spot on one of the walls. "What do you see?" he asked.

Maggie looked closer and squinted. "It looks like a cross," she answered.

"The living quarters were so tight that each of the friars had an assigned place that Francis marked off by painting crosses on the wall," Thomas said.

"Wow, these guys were serious," Maggie whispered.

Bernard appeared at the door. "Maggie, follow me. I want to show you something else," he said.

I knew these guys had been to the hermitage a hundred times before, but seeing it through Maggie's eyes was bringing the place to life for them again.

Bernard led Maggie and the rest of us into another cave, where he clasped his hands behind his back and rocked back and forth on his heels. "This," he announced, "is called the Chapel of the Presepio."

"It's great," I said. It wasn't much different from the other caves we'd seen, but Bernard clearly thought it was special, so I thought it best to humor him.

Bernard grinned. "Do you know what happened on the spot where you're standing?"

I looked around for a clue. "I don't ha—"

"This was the site where the first live crèche scene and Nativity play were performed," he said.

"You're kidding," Maggie said.

Bernard said, "No, it's true. It happened right here in this chapel."

Our little group formed a horseshoe around Bernard as he told the story. "It was the day before Christmas in 1223. Francis told the villagers he wanted to do something special to celebrate Jesus' birth—he would hold a Christmas Mass outdoors. In those days, it was unheard of. The townspeople jumped into high gear clearing the site, while the local candle makers started making altar candles. Then Francis got another idea—they would re-create a manger scene, complete with live oxen and donkey. No one had ever heard of such a thing! Now the farmers ran off, arguing about whose livestock would star in the celebration. Then Francis walked around the village, picking a few of the locals to play the parts of Mary, Joseph, the shepherds, the angels, and the Magi. That night, when everything was ready, the entire town turned out. The evening was lit with candles and torches. The people sang matins and watched as the Nativity was reenacted right before their eyes. Francis sang the gospel reading and preached with so much passion about the miracle of God's willingness to visit us as an infant that some said they actually saw the baby doll's eyes open. For one night, Francis transformed Greccio into Bethlehem."

I was so swept up in Bernard's tale that I imagined myself as a small boy darting back and forth so that I could glimpse the Nativity scene through the legs of the adults. I smelled the smoke from the candles on the makeshift altar mixing with the odor of animals and damp hay. This wasn't the pristine Nativity scene I'd sung about in carols all my life. Francis was revealing to me the true nature of the Incarnation: the moment when the Divine collided with the crude ordinariness of our world. All my romantic notions of Jesus' birth fell like a curtain, revealing the beauty of its earthiness. I'd never think about it in the same way again.

"And that was the first crèche?" Maggie asked.

"That's right," Bernard answered.

A group of tourists were pushing and shoving at the door, waiting to get into the chapel. An irritated guide made shooing gestures at Bernard. Apparently, we'd outstayed our welcome.

"Let's go outside," Kenny whispered.

We walked out onto a stone patio overlooking the valley and looked down on the town of Greccio, shimmering in the afternoon sun. Off to the side were wide steps that hugged and wound around the side of a small church, where the six of us sat under the shade of a gnarled mulberry tree. Inside the sanctuary, we could dimly hear the sound of a pilgrimage group singing worship choruses. The songs were old refrains from the seventies, but it didn't matter—the earnestness of their voices was touching. In the branches above our heads, a family of larks sang along with them.

"Chase, can you believe it?" Maggie said. "We stood in the very place where the first Christmas play happened! People must have been freaked."

Peter arranged his habit so he could sit more comfortably. "No one had ever seen that kind of spectacle," he said. "Most people went to Christmas Mass expecting to hear the Christmas story and a boring homily. If watches had been invented in those days, they'd have been staring at them the whole time. Francis wanted to wake up his audience to the true miracle of the birth of God. He avoided preaching doctrines and dogma, because he believed conversion happened more on the plane of experience than reason," Peter said.

Maggie winked at me. "You could take a lesson from Francis on that one," she said. Before I could open my mouth, she turned to me again and said, "No offense."

I smiled. "None taken," I said.

"The goal of Francis's preaching was simple. He wanted people to have shalom," Bernard said.

"You mean peace?" Maggie asked.

"Yes, but more than peace. Shalom is a deep harmony with the universe," Bernard said. "When sin entered the world, it ruptured the friendship we'd once had with God, with other people, with ourselves, with our bodies, and with the environment. Our spiritual, social, psychological, physical, and ecological relationships were fractured. Francis preached a gospel that was holistic. He wanted his hearers to have all those torn dimensions of their lives repaired. Conversion was about being reconciled and restored in every aspect of life. For Francis, that could only happen through the blood of Jesus, living by the words of Scripture and conforming our lives to the gospel."

"Francis was everything medieval preachers weren't," Kenny added. "For starters, he was authentic. He spoke about the only thing he knew—his own life. He'd say, 'Here's how Jesus met me in my sinfulness and how he can meet you in yours.' It was autobiography, not lecture."

"In the Middle Ages, sermons were delivered in Latin," Bernard continued, "but Francis insisted on speaking in the new Italian dialect so ordinary people could understand him. He filled his sermons with stories and metaphors. If he wanted you to know that bad company leads to bad habits, he'd stick his hand in a bucket of tar and pull it out so you could see it for yourself. If he wanted you to see that the love of money was the root of all evil, he'd have one of his friars drop coins out of his mouth into a pile of horse dung. And if he couldn't figure out how to say something with words, he'd pick up an instrument and sing it. He was so animated that people called him the 'living tongue.' Instead of the gloomy preaching that prevailed in those days, Francis's sermons were hilarious."

"Best of all, he commanded the friars to keep their sermons brief because the Lord himself kept his words short on earth," Kenny said.

Maggie poked me in the side. "You ought to try being short," she said.

"Very funny," I said, gently bumping Maggie with my shoulder.

"Now that I think about it, *preaching* isn't the best word for what Francis did. *Dialoguing* is a better word," Peter said. "In the Middle Ages, most preaching was pretty manipulative. It was all about the threat of damnation, hell, and judgment. That's how the church kept people in line and protected its power base. Clerics wanted people to believe the church held the keys to heaven, and that there was no hope of being saved without the church's help. Francis wanted no part of that. He was always courteous and respectful and spoke endlessly about the mercy and kindness of God—a God who was willing to enter human history and rescue us, a God who was intimate, not distant and aloof. His message really was 'good news' to people who were taught there were six degrees of separation between God and their wretched lives."

Thomas cleared his throat. "A truly great preacher isn't someone with a seminary degree who explains the gospel; it's someone who *is* the gospel. Francis gave away every possession he owned because he wanted people to see that it was possible to trust Jesus for everything. He walked barefoot everywhere, kissed the lesions of lepers, and bathed them so they'd know the love of God. In the middle of winter he gave the clothes off his back to people who were freezing to death, and thanked them for the chance to do it. He walked the talk, and everyone knew it. He could have stood in front of a crowd and read the phone book and people would have thrown their lives at the foot of the cross." Thomas said.

Kenny smiled.

"Francis was more than an entertaining street preacher. He didn't want to win people to faith through theological arguments or by reasoning with them. His way of evangelizing people was through the example of his own life. That's what gave his simple words so much gravity and impact. His life was his theology. He once said, 'It is no use walking anywhere to preach unless our walking is our preaching.' He taught the friars that preaching the good news was useless unless they *were* the good news. 'Preach as you go!' was one of his favorite sayings."

Maggie yawned. She suddenly looked very tired.

"I think our Maggie is done for the day. Let's go home, shall we?" Peter asked.

✝ ✝ ✝

The guys were quiet during the drive back to Assisi. Peter played a tape of Puccini's *Tosca* while Maggie laid her head on Thomas's shoulder and dozed. We arrived at the friary a little after five o'clock.

Maggie's eyes were still half closed. "I'd still like to take a little nap. Is that OK?" Maggie asked me.

"Sure. Dinner afterward?"

She stifled a yawn. "Yeah, wake me in an hour, or I won't be able to sleep later on," she said.

Maggie went to her room, and I walked upstairs to the main office. Bernard had arranged for me to use the friary's computer so I wouldn't have to keep walking over to the Internet café to check my e-mail. Unfortunately, it was a dial-up connection, and it took forever to download my stuff.

One e-mail was from Carla. She'd discovered that a new bassoonist in the symphony was a Christian. He told her about a good church in Rome, as well as a Bible study that attracted a lot of artists and musicians. He offered to take her to both. "I really feel like God is up to something in my life," she wrote. "Meeting you and this bassoonist in the same month can't be a coincidence. Don't you think someone's trying to tell me something?"

The next e-mail was from Ed, asking if I'd read the one he'd sent earlier. The elders wanted to know if I could come back sometime in the next week. Clearly, they were getting jittery.

The last e-mail was particularly intriguing. It was from Chip.

Dear Chase,

Hello! Or should I say, "Buongiorno"? I hope your time in Italy is going great and that you're getting some time to think and rest. You don't need to worry about things here at the church. I asked one of our adult volunteers to run the senior high program while I fill in for you, and things are running smoothly (although we miss you!). I do have one small question. The firm that audits the church's financials

*has been here closing out the books. They have a few questions about
the pastor's discretionary account. They say you wrote three checks
to yourself last year totaling $2,000 and want to know what they
were for. Of course I assured them you would never do anything that
was financially improper but they still want an explanation. Given
all that's happened I thought it would be smart to go straight to the
finance committee and the elders about their concerns. If word got out
that the auditors were nervous about something you'd done, I didn't
want them to be the last to know.*

*I know that everyone is anxious for you to come back next week.
Should I get someone to pick you up at the airport?*

Can't wait to see you, dude.

Chip

+ + +

"See, I told you he was a snake," Maggie said. I'd gotten a table at
the Grand Hotel Assisi. I couldn't afford it, but I wanted Maggie's
first meal in Assisi to be top-drawer. I had printed Chip's e-mail
and given it to her to read over dinner.

"He didn't need to go to the finance committee or the elders
first," she said. "He could've e-mailed you directly and asked
what those checks were for. I'm telling you, that boy wants your
job," she said, jabbing her index finger at me. "By the way, what's
the pastor's discretionary account?"

"It's a fund the elders gave me to help members in need. There
are only two people other than me who are authorized to know
where the money goes — the church treasurer and the auditor."

Maggie poured a glass of Pellegrino. "It's not that I don't trust
you, but why *did* you write those checks?"

I debated whether I could tell her in a way that wouldn't
breach anyone's confidentiality. "A member of our staff needed to
see a psychiatrist for depression but couldn't afford it. This person

was afraid that if anyone saw their name in the ledger, they'd start to ask questions. I gave this staff member the money out of my own pocket."

"And then you reimbursed yourself," Maggie said, putting two and two together. "You kept some kind of receipt, right?"

"In my desk at the condo."

She threw up her hands. "Case closed."

"Yes and no. Now Chip's planted doubts in people's minds about my integrity," I said. "It looks like you were right about him."

"So now what?"

"I'll e-mail Ed and tell him I have backup documentation for the checks. Unfortunately, it's probably too late for damage control," I said.

Maggie took a sip of sparkling water. "What are you going to tell him about coming back?"

I thought for a moment. "Today's Thursday. I'll tell him I'm coming back on Monday, so he can set up a meeting with the elders for Wednesday. I'm not looking forward to it." I felt an uncomfortable weight on my chest.

"I'll change my reservations so I can go back with you."

"Maggie, don't do that. You've never been to Europe before. You can't leave without seeing Rome," I said.

Maggie shook her head. "You're going back to a hornet's nest. You'll need all the support you can get."

Maggie had turned out to be an incredible friend, and I wondered if I deserved her devotion. I looked at her face in the glow of the candle on the table. Every careworn line around her eyes told the story of wisdom she'd earned the hard way. I was lucky to know her. I placed my hand on hers. "Thanks, Maggie," I said.

The waiter brought our food, and Maggie dove in. Every so often, she closed her eyes and made sounds like she was in ecstasy.

"What are you going to tell the elders?" she asked when dessert and coffee arrived.

We were sitting next to floor-to-ceiling French doors overlooking the valley. The last vestiges of light had turned the tips of the tall brown grasses a gentle purple and blue.

"When I left, I loved Jesus, but I was tired of Christianity," I said. "I tried to blame everything on the whole Christian subculture—but that isn't fair. Here, I've learned that no one is my problem but me. Francis never judged the church, even when he didn't like what it was doing. What right do I have to judge it? Spiritually, I just want something more." I took a bite of the hotel's famous creamy ricotta cheesecake. I could actually hear my cholesterol levels climbing.

"All fine and good, but what are you going to *tell* them when they ask you what's next?" Maggie asked.

"I'm still not sure. But I'd like to ask you a favor," I said.

Maggie tamped the end of her cigarette on the back of her hand. "Name it," she replied, lighting it.

"I'd like you to read my journal."

Maggie was silent. "Are you crazy? I wouldn't show my journal to anyone. I told Gina that if I ever died, she had to get to my journals first and burn them."

I took my journal out of my bag and handed it to her. "There's a lot in here that might surprise you, especially since I'm your pastor."

Maggie caressed the cover. "Are you kidding, with my history?" she said. "I've got more luggage than Samsonite and Coach put together."

"There's a lot in there about Francis too."

"Would it be OK if I mailed it to Regina? She could print the juicier parts in the church newsletter."

I laughed. "Why not?" I said. "It couldn't get me into any more trouble than I'm in right now."

Maggie clutched my journal to her chest. "Seriously, I'm honored. It's safe with me," she said.

"I know." For the first time in my life, I was sharing my pilgrimage with someone else.

✝ ✝ ✝

Journal Entry:
The Friary, 11:30 p.m.

Dear Francis,

The plot is thickening. Maggie fell out of the sky today. Chip wants my corner office. Next week I have to journey home. Things are getting interesting, and it's probably just the beginning.

Brother James (a friar at San Rufino) gave me a little book about you called St. Francis and the Foolishness of God. It's great. Here's a section that moved me: "It is clear that today, just as in the time of Francis, the Spirit is raising up countercultural Christian communities at a time when God's people most need the support and challenge such gatherings can provide. This 'community of communities,' as it is called, strives to live as if the priorities of modern society did not hold sway; as if the values of God's Reign were already operative in modern society ... The experience of Francis, though distant in history, provides a ray of hope for this new movement. Today, too, there is a need to 'rebuild my church,' and the rebuilding promises to take place in and through this movement of communities ... In communities we join with scores of faith-filled men and women to live the great political and theological 'as ifs.' Politically we live as if our nation were still true to its foundational documents of liberty and justice for all; as if people mattered in themselves and not for their economic or social status; as if consumerism and the shopping mall did not determine the meaning of our lives ... Living these 'as ifs' in the midst of community creates the prophetic possibility at a local level, the space for modeling how things could be, ought to be, and will be one day."

I grew up in a faith that was highly individualistic. We talked about personal—personal evangelism, personal relationships with Christ, and personal devotions. We enjoyed "fellowship," but we never talked much about the power of community and how it could change individual lives and the world. This idea of the church being an "as if" people who live together like the kingdom were "already here in its fullness" is inspiring to me.

Here's one last quote: "In fact, Francis has been called the 'first Protestant' because of his reform from within the body of the church. He saw such reform as always necessary, given the frailty and sinfulness of a human institution ... He and his communities walked a most difficult path: remaining in a sin-filled church while offering her a prophetic challenge. He and the first communities served as a constant critique to the church, living as they did the gospel without gloss, a witness that called the entire household of faith to do the same. To the church's ostentation, inattention to the poor, neglect of pastoral responsibilities, complicity in the violence of the state, and general situation of decline, the emerging Franciscan movement offered both a strong condemnation and a corrective. It was the communal example of Francis and his followers, rather than rhetoric, which offered the critique and provided the challenge."

That last sentence is very convicting. Francis, you changed the church (in fact, you re-evangelized it)—not through being critical, but through forming a community that confounded it. For the last few years, I've been a self-righteous critic of the church and all of Christendom, and I need to give that up. Sister Irene told me the other day that "no one else is your problem but you." Maybe I should try to live the "gospel without gloss" and keep my mouth shut?

Your friend,
Chase

PS: I gave my journal to Maggie so I'm using my laptop to write you. Don't be put off by technology.

X

One goes more quickly to heaven
from a hut than from a palace.
SAINT FRANCIS OF ASSISI

I SPENT MUCH OF FRIDAY MORNING ON THE PHONE WITH ALITA-
lia trying to change Maggie's ticket. Every time I thought we
had things worked out, the ticket agent found another absurdly
obscure airline regulation that required Maggie to purchase a new
ticket. After two hours, three blasé supervisors, and a fistful of
Advil, I hoisted the white flag. I didn't tell Maggie, but I had to
fork over $735 to get the two of us on the same flight. Afterward,
I sent an e-mail to Ed letting him know I'd be back late Sunday
night—but not that Maggie was with me. News of my traveling
around Italy with a woman from the congregation would have
been fatal. He texted back, saying he could probably pull together
an elders' meeting for Monday night. I had hoped to have more
time to prepare, but the elders were anxious.

Breaking the news to the guys was going to be difficult. I
owed it to Kenny to tell him first, but I wasn't looking forward
to it. I meandered upstairs to the guardian's office and could hear
Kenny on the phone, laughing and talking in Italian. I poked my
head around the door, and he signaled me to come in. I sat and
shuffled magazines on the coffee table, looking for something in
English.

Kenny hung up and flopped into the chair across from me.
"So?" he asked smiling.

"Kenny, I'm leaving on Sunday night," I said.

The smile fell from Kenny's face. He gazed intently into my eyes. He was taking an inventory, trying to discern if I was ready for what lay ahead. "How do you feel?" he asked.

"Scared," I said.

"Do you know what you're going to say to people?"

"Not yet."

Kenny nodded. "You will."

"Kenny, I can't begin—"

Kenny put his finger to his lips to shush me. "Not yet. We'll have plenty of time for good-byes later on. Let's go tell the others," he said, standing. I grabbed his outstretched hand and he yanked me out of the chair.

We walked down the hallway and out onto the second-floor veranda. Peter and Bernard were sitting at a wrought-iron patio table playing chess; a large green umbrella in the center of the table shaded them from the blinding glare of the morning sun. Thomas was standing in front of an easel, painting the Rocca Maggiore fortress that sat on the hillside above us. For a smock, he wore a red plaid shirt that looked older than me. It was laundry day, so they were all in their civvies.

"I see you've all kicked your habits," I said. No one bothered to look up.

Peter moved his rook. "That's hysterical, Chase. Who writes your material?"

"Never heard that one before," Bernard muttered.

"Chase and Maggie are leaving us on Sunday night," Kenny announced.

Everyone stopped what they were doing and gawked at me as if I'd just run over their dog. A powerful bond had been forged among us in a short few weeks, during which we'd avoided the subject of our inevitable parting.

Bernard shot up from his seat. "But what about Maggie?"

"What about her?" I asked.

"She hasn't seen Rome!" he answered.

"She hasn't seen Rome?" the others cried in unison. This was beginning to sound like the chorus of a Gilbert & Sullivan opera.

"Well, she's decided—"

"That's unacceptable; it's bad form to come to Italy and not see Rome," Peter said indignantly. "Tell Maggie to pack this instant. Bernard, call the Residenza Madri Pie and reserve rooms."

Thomas took his easel apart. "Can I help?" he asked.

"Get our habits out of the dryer," Peter called over his shoulder as he hurried out the French doors.

Soon it was only Kenny and me on the veranda. He leaned on the chipped iron railing. "They don't want to say good-bye yet," he said.

I sighed. "We still have two full days," I said.

Kenny flicked his cigarette over the side and placed his hand on my shoulder. "Let's make them beautiful," he replied.

✢ ✢ ✢

Friday night sticks out in my memory as one of the most unforgettable nights of my life. We checked into the Madri Pie around five o'clock and agreed to meet in the lobby at seven for dinner. I called Carla to see if she was in town, but according to her answering machine, she was in Prague with the symphony until Tuesday. I left a message saying I was leaving Italy but I'd be in touch. When I got down to the lobby, it was clear that Maggie had taken charge of the troops. Rome is a city of passion, eternal beauty, and pulsating life. Maggie's engine was primed, and she was waiting on the tarmac. She wore tight black jeans and an open, ribbed violet shirt over a black tank top that highlighted her belly-button piercing. At first, the guys came down in their habits, but Maggie ordered them back to their rooms to change. They came back wearing street clothes that would have sent Armani into paroxysms of despair. Maggie was holding a travel guide that she'd found in her room and had already circled the places she wanted to go.

She gathered the guys into a huddle. "When was the last time you men went dancing?" she asked.

They all shuffled and glanced around at each other.

"Right after the war," Thomas said finally.

Peter laughed. "Which one?"

"You don't want to know," Kenny answered.

"Tonight may be my last night in Rome, so I plan on making it count," Maggie warned, closing the guidebook.

The trendiest clubs in Rome are found around Monte Testaccio and along the nearby Via Ostiense. We gorged on a magnificent dinner while watching Italian hipsters prowl the streets, waiting for the clubs to open. Maggie entertained us by telling off-color jokes in such a loud voice that people at the surrounding tables were laughing along with us.

Around ten o'clock, she took us to a dance club called Alpheus that had four separate dance floors, each playing a different kind of music. The bass frequencies pumping out of the subwoofers were so concussive that it felt like someone was punching me in the chest with the business end of a shovel. At first I wasn't sure how the guys would respond. To my surprise, they plunged into the moment with abandon. They wanted this to be the best night of Maggie's life, and I loved them for it. The whole scene was like a sketch from *Saturday Night Live*—four Franciscan friars dancing under strobe lights with an ex-con to the sounds of Snoop Dogg. Maggie even managed to talk Thomas into dancing with her for half a song. Bernard, however, was the big hit of the night. You couldn't pry him off the floor. There he was, drenched in sweat, twirling and shaking his titanic rear end while the rest of us doubled over with laughter. He looked like he was going to bawl when we told him it was time to leave.

By the time we got back to the Madri Pie it was well past one o'clock. Thomas, Maggie, and I rode the elevator together up to our rooms. As he was about to get off on his floor, Thomas held the door open and turned around. "I'd like to take you somewhere in the morning," he said.

Maggie and I looked at each other.

"OK," Maggie said hesitantly. "What time?"

"Don't worry. I'll come and wake you," he said, releasing the door and walking into the dimly lit hallway.

✝ ✝ ✝

Four hours later, Maggie and I sat like zombies in the backseat of a cab. Thomas had knocked on our doors at five. If we'd known this was his idea of "morning," we might have given him a different answer.

As we drove Rome's empty, rain-drenched streets, Thomas was evasive about where we were going. One thing was clear—we weren't going to a fancy breakfast spot. Decrepit buildings, abandoned cars, and trash-strewn sidewalks rushed by my window.

The cab pulled up in front of an old church attached by a glass breezeway to a modern-looking annex. A motley group of people milled around outside. Some sat with their backs against the side of the building, half asleep—while others gathered in small groups, smoking and talking. If the spirit of resignation were a smell, the place would have stunk. We walked through the crowd to the building, and Thomas rang the bell. Through the glass door, I could see a woman approaching down the hallway, holding a wad of keys. When she saw Thomas, her face lit up and she couldn't open the deadbolts fast enough.

"*Tomaso!*" she cried, throwing her arms around Thomas's small frame and kissing him on both cheeks.

"Angelina, these are my friends," Thomas said in English. "We've come to help."

Angelina hugged us warmly. "Wonderful," she said. "Where are you from?"

"Connecticut," I replied. "Just outside New York City."

Angelina placed her hand on my shoulder and glared at me playfully. "You're not a Yankees fan, are you?"

"I'm afraid so," I laughed.

"Too bad. I'm from Cleveland, so you're in Indian country," she said.

Angelina and Thomas spoke in rapid-fire Italian while Maggie and I traipsed behind. A flickering fluorescent bulb made an honorable but feeble attempt to light the dingy passage. The ambiance would have been completely depressing if it hadn't been for the smell of warm bread and freshly brewed coffee wafting languidly down the hall.

"Where are we, exactly?" Maggie asked, looking around for clues.

"You are at the Comunitá del Poverello d'Assisi. We're a soup kitchen," Angelina replied over her shoulder.

We turned a corner and entered an industrial-sized kitchen where a crowd of people was busily preparing breakfast. Volunteer cooks and servers shouted with delight when they saw Thomas. They put down their work and wiped their hands on their aprons so they could hug him. When Thomas had greeted everyone, Angelina sat the three of us at a table in the empty dining hall and poured us some coffee.

"You're a long way from Cleveland," Maggie said.

Angelina nodded and blew on her coffee to cool it. "I came here as a foreign exchange student in 1968 and never went back."

"Why not?" I asked.

"I met another student named Giacomo Cavaccone at the university's Catholic youth club. He invited me to a group that met in his apartment to talk about how to live the gospel. We studied Francis's life and decided it was hard to be a Christian and not be with the poor. So we began wandering through the slums of Rome making friends with homeless people and feeding them. We didn't know it would turn into all of this," she said, looking around the room.

"Is Giacomo here?" Maggie asked, peering into the kitchen.

"He's visiting one of our houses in Nicaragua," Angelina replied.

"Nicaragua?" I asked.

"We have houses in forty-six countries. There are ten thousand lay volunteers," Angelina answered.

Maggie whistled with amazement.

"How do you know Thomas?" I asked.

Angelina touched Thomas on the hand. "Everyone knows Thomas," she said.

"Tomaso, come join us in the kitchen!" someone yelled. Thomas excused himself.

Angelina picked up the carafe and poured us more coffee. "So, you're on a pilgrimage," she said.

I shook my head and laughed. It seemed that everywhere I went in Italy, people had been given an advance briefing of my life. "Yes," I replied. "We're going home Sunday night."

"You've come to the right place to end your trip," she said. "To know Francis, you have to know the poor."

"Angelina, we're opening the doors," a man called.

Angelina picked two aprons off an adjoining table and tossed them to us. She tied her apron strings. "Time to welcome Jesus," she said.

For the next two hours, Maggie and I helped serve breakfast to what felt like a never-ending stream of homeless people. They were the ragtag of humanity—the mentally ill, drug addicts, the forgotten elderly, and children in tattered clothes running from table to table. Some of the guests were grateful; others were unappreciative and refused to look us in the eye.

Maggie was in her element. A tired mother was only too glad to let Maggie hold her baby. Maggie walked around the dining hall bouncing the giggling child playfully in the crook of her arm. Even though she didn't know a word of Italian, she worked the room like she was running for mayor. Wherever she went, peals of laughter followed.

Angelina continued our conversation in bits and pieces as we placed food and drink on the tables. "Francis used to say he was married to Lady Poverty," she said, raising her voice over the din.

I used a corner of my apron to wipe sweat from my face. "What does that mean?"

"Poverty was the cornerstone of his ministry."

The two of us began clearing dishes to make room for the next round of guests. Angelina continued. "There's a metaphor in the story of Francis publicly stripping himself naked before Bishop Guido and returning the money he'd stolen from his father. It symbolized his rejection of his culture's manic pursuit of wealth and status. He didn't want anything to do with the materialistic, middle-class world he'd been raised in. From that moment, he committed himself to living a life of poverty and serving the poor."

She disappeared into the crowd, carrying a tray of dirty dishes. As I sponged off the table, I thought about what she'd said. You couldn't read anything about Francis that didn't talk about his devotion to poverty. He actually despised money. The only requirement for entering the Franciscan Order was to sell everything you had and give it to the poor. Angelina soon returned with fresh plates and began resetting the table.

"Francis's devotion to poverty sounds over-the-top to me," I said, folding napkins.

"For him, it was a way of completely identifying with Jesus," she said.

"But even Jesus and the disciples carried a purse to provide for themselves."

"True. But Francis believed that the Incarnation itself was Jesus' way of embracing poverty—the Son of God coming to earth to be born in a stable and die on a cross."

"Yes, but isn't living a life of voluntary poverty a little ... impractical?" I asked.

Angelina stopped working and laughed out loud. "When did following Jesus become practical?" she asked.

Maggie interrupted our conversation. "Who's that guy over there?" she asked. Leaning against a wall was a small man performing magic tricks for a group of children. He seemed to be reveling in the mayhem. His appearance was no different from all the other people in the room—his simple gray pants and old black sweatshirt emblazoned with the mascot of an American university looked as if they had been picked out of a bin of donated clothes. Around his tiny waist was a necktie that had been drafted into use as a belt. I wouldn't have noticed him if Maggie hadn't pointed him out. Thomas, however, shadowed him as he moved around the room.

Angelina shrugged. "That's Umberto. He's a regular around here."

Maggie cocked her head and stared at him. "He looks so familiar."

Angelina knelt and hugged a small boy as he passed. "Let's hurry and finish these dishes. There's still a lot to do."

✝ ✝ ✝

Angelina drove the mobile soup kitchen truck, while Thomas, Maggie, and I rode in the rear cabin with the supplies. Through the back windows, we could see a second truck behind us, filled with more volunteers and food.

Every day, members of the community go out and bring meals to homeless people who can't get to the soup kitchen on their own steam.

Maggie and I were tired but exhilarated; our time with the guests at the community house had been energizing.

"Francis loved poverty because it helped him spiritually," Thomas said. He'd overheard my conversation with Angelina and wanted to add his two cents. "There is a law in physics that applies to the soul. No two objects can occupy the same space at the same time; one thing must displace another. If your heart's crammed tight with material things and a thirst for wealth, there's no space left for God. Francis wanted a void in his life that could only be filled with Jesus. Poverty wasn't a burden for him—it was a pathway to spiritual freedom."

Maggie nodded. "My first year of sobriety was hell. Didn't have anything but the clothes on my back. Whenever I complained, my sponsor used to say, 'We never know that Jesus is enough until Jesus is all we have left.' In a weird way, I kind of miss those days."

Thomas's eyes sparkled. "Francis read the Bible the way a child would—completely trusting. So when Jesus said to not worry about your life, what you'll eat or drink or wear, Francis said, 'OK, I won't.' And this was the beginning of his love affair with poverty."

I'd always felt conflicted when I read Jesus' teachings about money and materialism, especially the part about selling everything we own and giving it to the poor. I'd grown up in a very privileged home and attended the finest schools. Now I wore nice clothes, drove a Volvo, and ministered in one of the wealthiest communities in the world. Bumping around in the back of the truck, I thought about a commercial I'd seen on TV for an expensive sports car. It showed the car elegantly maneuvering around hairpin turns and roaring to a stop just in front of the camera. Then the announcer's voice said, "You can't buy happiness. It is, however, available for lease." I knew I'd been co-opted by the culture of materialism I lived in, but getting out of it seemed impossible. Picking pesto off pasta seemed easier.

Angelina pulled over and stopped at the curb. She opened the double doors, and we hopped out the back. She pulled together all the volunteers and began giving directions in Italian.

Thomas translated for us. "Some of us will stay here and get the food ready. The rest of us will go out and check on people. Remember to be respectful and courteous to everyone, regardless of how they treat you. Answer any rudeness with kindness, as Francis would."

"Why don't you three come with me?" Angelina said, marching off.

She led us down a narrow side street. Between garbage dumpsters in back alleys were large cardboard boxes that served as homes for the city's poorest residents. I'd seen makeshift neighborhoods like this in New York City, but this one was really squalid. Every now and then, Angelina or Thomas would kneel in front of a box and ask the person inside if they wanted to talk or come to the soup truck. Some would come out and greet us, others eyed us suspiciously, and some weren't coherent enough to respond one way or the other. Maggie was quieter than usual; her eyes darted in every direction.

As we turned a corner, we saw an old refrigerator carton lying on its side. Two feet wearing worn-out tennis shoes stuck out of the opening.

"This is where Isabella and Grazia live," Angelina whispered. She knelt in front of the box and waved Maggie and me over. Thomas stood to one side and watched. "Isabella, I've brought food and friends," she said gently.

There was a woman inside, lying down. Her eyes were glazed over, and she was barely able to acknowledge our presence. Sitting cross-legged next to her was a young girl, maybe ten years old, clutching a small bag of potato chips. Her nose was running and she was shivering. Her dark brown eyes warned us not to come too close.

"That little girl is sick," Maggie said with concern.

Angelina nodded. "It's been cold at night."

Maggie held out her arms. "Can you come to me, sweetheart?" she asked.

Grazia backed further into the box and shook her head.

"Please, I promise not to hurt you," Maggie said, her voice sounding more constricted.

Grazia looked down at her mother as if checking to make sure she was still all right. Then, hesitantly, she came out of the box on her hands and knees and stood before Maggie. Maggie licked her own fingers and wiped the grime off Grazia's cheeks, gently chiding her for getting so dirty; then using her fingers like a comb she tried to neaten the girl's hair. It was as if the rest of us were gone now—there was no one else in Maggie's world but Grazia.

"All you need is a hot bath, a warm meal, and a good night's rest, and you'll be better tomorrow." Maggie said. Grazia gazed through Maggie.

Maggie inspected Grazia's hand and found a cut. "This is getting infected. We'll need to clean it and put some ointment on it," she said. Though Maggie spoke now in a louder voice, trying to get Grazia's attention, the girl still seemed disconnected, staring trancelike into the distance.

"Can you hear me, honey?" Maggie asked more loudly, almost angrily.

Grazia suddenly focused on Maggie. She cocked her head sideways and frowned—then her face relaxed, and her slender form melted into Maggie. Her lifeless eyes and loose-boned body radiated a weariness none of us could understand—except, apparently, Maggie, who buried her face so deeply in Grazia's filthy hair that the sound of her plaintive sobs was muted.

Maggie had once told me that when her drug problem had been at its worst, she and Iris were homeless, ping-ponging from one shelter to another. It had never occurred to me that they had probably spent nights on the street as well. Now she was holding a ghost, the memory of a daughter who had traveled the hardest roads with her, only to die when the winds of fortune shifted in their favor. Grazia was a sacrament, a momentary point of contact with Iris.

Isabella struggled to sit up. She shook her head, straining to come out of a drug-induced haze. She was disoriented, but her eyes flashed with anger when she saw Grazia in Maggie's arms. She reached out to her daughter, but Maggie held on tighter.

"Maggie, you have to let Grazia go," Angelina said quietly.

Maggie closed her eyes. "I won't. Not this time," she said.

"Please, Maggie," Angelina said, more firmly.

Maggie started, then looked up, surprised, as if she'd been rudely awakened from a dream. With mournful resignation, she slowly released the little girl to her mother. Then she stood and wiped her eyes with the back of her hand. "God's a maniac," she said.

Angelina took Maggie's hand, and the two of them walked up the street together. I turned to follow them, but Thomas touched my shoulder and pointed at another box next to Isabella and Grazia's. Whoever lived inside it kept it as neat as possible. There was a neatly folded brown blanket, and the pavement in front of it looked as if it had been recently swept. Just inside the opening was a small jar with a lone geranium sitting in brownish water. "That's where Umberto lives," Thomas said.

✝ ✝ ✝

After we returned to the community house, Angelina said she had one more ministry for us to see. "It's the one I'm most proud of," she said.

"I won't be joining you, Angelina. I promised to meet someone here," Thomas said.

Angelina used her keyless remote to open the car doors for us. "Should we pick you up when we're done?" she asked.

Thomas waved us on. "No, no, I'll find my way back to the hotel," he said.

As we pulled away, I looked through the rear window and saw Umberto emerge from the shadow of a tall oak. He and Thomas linked arms and disappeared around the corner of the building.

"What does *Il Poverello* mean?" Maggie asked, referring to the community's name.

"It means 'Little Poor Man.' It was one of Francis's nicknames," Angelina said.

"What's the story behind it?" Maggie asked.

"In the Middle Ages, the church had lost credibility because it was pursuing wealth and power like everyone else. When people compared the way Francis and the friars lived with the lifestyle of the culture and church, they said, 'These guys are the genuine articles. They're living proof that the gospels are true. Jesus really is all you need to find meaning and joy in life.' Francis instructed his friars never to criticize rich people or clerics who wore ornate clothes and expensive jewelry—but they didn't need to. The way they lived served as an indictment against others. Many of the first Franciscans were aristocrats who sold everything they had to follow *Il Poverello*. Francis, the playboy from Assisi, inspired them to see that living acquisitively wasn't what life was about. We could use more of that kind of witness today."

"What do you mean?" Maggie asked.

Angelina sighed. "As you know, the United States is the wealthiest country in the history of the world. We represent only about 5 percent of the world's population, yet we consume 40 percent of its resources. We're demonically possessed by materialism and hyper-consumption. It's true in the wealthiest sectors of almost every other country as well. Unfortunately, Christians are as caught up in the system as everyone else. The twenty-first century is perpetrating the lie that was popular in the thirteenth century—the more you have, the happier you'll be," Angelina said.

Maggie frowned, puzzled. "Christians don't believe that."

Angelina chuckled. "We *say* we don't believe it, but our lives betray us. The church is as co-opted by money today as it was in the thirteenth century. Our next-door neighbors must look at us and think, *You Christians say you're citizens of a different kingdom, yet you're just as consumed by malls, money, cars, clothes, vacations, and homes as we are. What's the deal?* Why should anyone take our gospel seriously as long we continue to serve two masters? A faith that doesn't speak out against the sick assumptions of its culture is really no faith at all; it's just religion," she said.

I was reminded of one of my seminary professors, who had told us of the radical economics of the early church and that it experienced such dramatic growth in its nascent years because of them. No one had ever seen a community of people so lavishly generous with each other and with the poor—people liberated from the need to find meaning and security in Mammon.

"So what are we supposed to do—sell everything we have and give it to the poor?" I asked. The question wasn't combative; it was an earnest plea for advice.

In heavy traffic, Angelina stopped at a red light near the city center. "What if we started by repenting of our materialism and living more simply? I think we'd change the world in a heartbeat."

"I guess Francis would have been turned off by the prosperity gospel," I said facetiously.

"Don't even go there," she replied, pulling into a parking lot surrounded by a chain-link fence topped with razor wire. After we got out of the car, she double-checked to make sure the doors were locked. Then she winked at us. "You can never be too careful in this neighborhood. I've had two radios torn out of my dashboard here."

This stop turned out to be the community's home for men dying of AIDS. When I discovered where we were, I was surprised by how apprehensive I felt. I'd spent a lot of time around dying people, so that wasn't it. Maybe I was self-conscious about being around gay men and needle addicts.

"Most of the men who live here have no one to take care of them," Angelina said. "Their families have disowned them, and their friends have stopped visiting. We help them die with dignity, and hopefully they see Jesus in us."

The house was quiet except for a cat meowing in some faraway room. The three of us walked up the stairs to the second floor. Through open doors, we could see men in different stages of illness. Some were propped up in bed reading; others slept. At the top of the third-floor landing, a petite young woman with close-cropped hair and a beaming smile was waiting for us.

"This is Eva. She's a volunteer in training from one of our houses in Germany," Angelina said.

Eva shook my hand. "You've come just in time. We need to give the men baths," she said.

"Maggie, why don't you go downstairs and look in on some of the men? They love visitors," Angelina said. I knew we'd soon hear laughter coming from the floor below.

"Can I go with her?" I asked.

Angelina placed her hand on my arm. "We could use you up here," she said.

My heart was beating like a drum against my rib cage, just at the idea of giving a man a bath. I scrambled for a reason why I couldn't possibly help, but I wasn't fast enough. Angelina took my hand, and we went into a room where a young man lay on a bed, staring blankly at the ceiling.

"*Buongiorno*, Amadeo," Angelina said. "I've brought a friend today." Angelina removed the blanket that covered Amadeo's body. He was a naked stick, mute, his almond-shaped eyes filled with that pitiable mixture of panic and confusion. His pallid skin hung flaccidly — he must have been six feet tall once, but now he surely weighed less than a hundred pounds. I felt a rush of both shock and sadness. I looked at Angelina for help, and she smiled at me reassuringly.

"Let's put Amadeo in the tub," she said, as she repeated in Italian so that he and I would both know what we were doing next.

Eva dipped her hands into the water to make sure it was the right temperature, while Angelina and I lifted Amadeo. I tenderly placed my hands under his shoulder blades. They felt like sharp-edged clamshells cruelly implanted in his upper back. I was afraid his skin would tear like tissue in my grip. The bones of his pelvis stuck out through his skin like six-guns in flesh holsters.

We lowered him slowly into the bath; the steam that moved across the water parted as his body passed through it. Amadeo winced as the open sores on his body made contact with the tepid water. Angelina spoke to him soothingly while sponging off his brittle frame.

She handed me a rag. "Would you mind washing his genitals," she asked evenly.

I was speechless. The stick-man looked at me as if to say, "What will you choose to do now?"

There is a tensile surface on water that's always fascinated me. I've ruminated before about that infinitesimally thin layer of resistance when preparing for baptisms. Is the water giving the candidate one last chance to go back, a last-minute opportunity to pull away and say no to the intense yet life-giving drowning that lies ahead? Or is it a reminder that there really is a separation between this fallen world and the next?

As I pushed against my revulsion and plunged the sponge beneath the water, I thought of it again but refused its invitation to hold back. I'd passed through a border into the depths and found I could still breathe there. My terror and embarrassment was replaced by peace, edging toward sublime joy.

"Did you know that Francis had a phobic aversion to lepers?" Angelina asked, continuing to wash Amadeo.

I wrung the water out of my rag. "I've read about it," I said quietly.

"He was so disgusted by them that whenever he saw one, he'd cover his mouth and nose and run away. One day, he was riding his horse on the outskirts of Assisi and saw a leper. He was tempted to take off in the other direction, but then he heard Jesus telling him to get off his horse and kiss the leper. He did, and it was a breakthrough moment in his conversion."

Angelina and I lifted Amadeo out of the tub and placed him on the bed, where Eva had placed fresh towels. We patted him dry and gingerly dabbed ointment on his sores. Amadeo closed his eyes, and his expression softened into something resembling peace. I wasn't sure which was the more soothing to him—the cleansing, the salve, or the sensation of people touching him.

When we were finished, Eva put a warm fleece blanket over him. Angelina put her face close to his. "Good-bye, my friend. I will look in on you tomorrow." Amadeo opened his eyes and stared at her. His lips moved, but no words came—only the sound of air passing over his vocal chords. Angelina kissed him on the forehead.

While we were walking down the stairs, Maggie came out of one of the rooms and met us in the hall. I must have looked dazed because she looked sideways at me. "What happened up there?" she asked

"I think I became a Christian," I said.

Journal Entry:
Residenza Madri Pie, 4:00 p.m.

Dear Francis,

I thought your fixation on poverty was part of that medieval Catholic thing—fanatical monks and ascetics beating their bodies and starving themselves in order to do penance. But that wasn't it. You chose a life of poverty because it created the optimal conditions for your

soul to mature. I confess that I'm a lifelong collaborator with the forces of materialism and consumerism. Is it possible to live in America and not be? If Angelina is right, though, I'm paying a high cost for it spiritually. On the back of one of the brochures from the Community of the Little Poor One, there's a quote taken from The Essentials of Mysticism by Evelyn Underhill: "Mystics know that possessions dissipate the energy which they need for other and more real things; that they must give up ownership, the verb 'to have,' if they are to attain the freedom which they seek, and the fullness of the verb 'to be.'"

God knows how much energy I expend on buying and maintaining all my material possessions. It's embarrassing to think about the energy I expend just thinking about buying stuff. I actually lease one of those self-storage lockers; it's packed with stuff I've accumulated over the years but can't fit into my condo. Is that a metaphor for my not-so-maturing soul—so filled with junk that it has no room for God?

I think Angelina's right. As long as Christians and the church continue colluding with the powers of consumerism and materialism, our witness is impeded. I won't be giving any lectures or sermons on it in the near future, though—I'm still the worst of sinners.

I fed poor people and bathed a man with AIDS today. It was a good day, Francis, a very good day.

Your friend,
Chase

I had just saved my journal entry and shut down my computer when Maggie burst into my hotel room. "We can do this!" she said. I nearly fell off my chair. "Do what?"

She thrust my journal into my hands. "This," she said.

✝ ✝ ✝

For an hour or more, Maggie and I wandered the streets of Rome and talked. She'd read through my journal twice and even taken notes.

"Chase, you have the blueprint for the church we want to be part of right here." Maggie was in front of me walking backward, waving my journal and talking a million miles an hour.

"Get real, Maggie," I said.

"You need to tell the elders about Francis—about his spirit, his ministry," she said.

I tried to grab my journal from her, but she pulled it away.

"Maggie, they wouldn't buy this stuff in a million years," I said.

"How do you know? Give them a little credit," she replied.

Maggie was more courageous than I was. For several nights in a row, I'd drifted off to sleep fantasizing about leading a church that based its ministry on the heart and life of Francis. Each time, though, I'd dismissed the idea as completely insane. Whoever heard of a conservative Protestant church adopting a Catholic saint's approach to living the Christian life—especially a saint who lived eight hundred years ago? It was ludicrous. And yet Maggie's enthusiasm for the idea began to charge me up.

"Let's pretend we wanted to do it. What would we do first?" I asked.

Maggie saw the crack in the door. "I'd put together a very well-thought-out presentation for the elders," she said.

"People will think I've lost my mind," I said.

Maggie grabbed my shoulders. "Chase, stop worrying about what other people think! You're thirty-nine years old. It's time to grow up."

I sat down on top of a wall surrounding one of the million marble fountains in Rome. The sound of gushing water enveloped me. Maggie was right again. Half the reason my life had blown up was that I didn't have the courage to stop reading off the "good boy—don't make any waves" script. I'd been afraid that, if I did, I'd end up disappointing people and they'd leave me. I had lived that way all my life—and it hadn't worked. I couldn't go back to living that way again.

"Well?"

For a moment I'd forgotten where I was. I looked at my watch. "It's six now. Let's see what we can get done tonight," I said.

When we got back to the hotel, we ordered two carafes of coffee and set up shop on the patio. All the books I'd accumulated on my pilgrimage were in piles on the table, teetering like ziggurat towers. For twelve straight hours, Maggie and I talked, compared ideas, argued, and wrote. The night was one long adrenaline rush. By seven o'clock on Sunday morning, we had a reasonable first draft of a document for the elders.

Maggie lit a cigarette; the crushed remnants of two other packs lay on the table. She held up a sheaf of papers. "This church would rock," she said.

I yawned and stretched. "Let's hope a few other people think so."

We went back to our rooms to catch a few hours of sleep. As I lay on the bed, a wave of dread washed over me. Sitting on the bedside table was a draft describing the church I wanted to lead, a church I could believe in again—the kind of Christian I wanted to become. What if people laughed?

"Don't even go there," I whispered.

I set my alarm clock and called Kenny. "Do you think we can pull the guys together at four o'clock?" I asked.

"I think so. What's up?"

"I want to tell them how much Francis has screwed up my life."

There was silence on the other end. "I'll make sure everyone's there," he answered.

✝ ✝ ✝

"Come on, what do you think?" I asked.

Maggie and I had spent two hours painting a picture for

Kenny, Bernard, Peter, and Thomas of a church that embraced the heart of Francis. We were like doctoral students defending their theses, except on steroids.

Peter spoke up first. "Chase and Maggie—I'm speechless. It's wonderful," he said.

"You've brought him to life in a new way," Bernard said.

Kenny stood and kissed me on the cheek. "Well done, son," he whispered in my ear. "And you!" he yelled at Maggie. "You are an angel sent by God."

"Hear, hear," they all cried.

Thomas nodded at me. That was all I needed from him.

We spent another half hour refining our ideas and brainstorming how to implement them. Peter was impressed that we had essentially contemporized the "Rule of 1223." Others added their two cents, but the overwhelming opinion was that our paper was a superb start.

"Look—if your elders don't like it, you can always come back here and become a friar," Bernard said.

Maggie howled. "I'd pay fifty bucks to see Chase in one of those habits."

"I hate to break this up, but we need to get you to the airport by nine o'clock," Kenny said.

"Do we have time for a farewell meal?" Bernard asked.

"Just what I had in mind," Kenny said. "Let's go to Mass."

✝ ✝ ✝

Kenny had a sense of the poetic. He took us to a six o'clock Mass in one of the side chapels at Saint John Lateran's. It was only fitting that our last stop would be at the site where the Franciscan Order had received its blessing from the pope to go forth and minister to the world. Maggie had been raised a Catholic, so none of the ritual was new to her, but I still had to watch what everyone else was doing and copy it. I actually thought I'd successfully fooled the celebrating priest and the twenty other people in the church into believing I knew what I was doing.

But when we knelt at the altar to receive Communion, all of my confidence quickly withered. When the elderly priest came to me, I held out my cupped hands to receive the Communion host. The old priest, however, suffered from a slight tremor in his hands, so I had to keep moving my own to try and position them under his to receive the round wafer. It was a comedy of errors. He moved left and I went right. He went right and I moved left. I began to panic.

Just when it looked like the exchange might end happily, the unthinkable happened. The wafer fell between the cracks of my coupled hands and hit the stone floor of the altar in front of me. It's hard to believe that something so small and light could make so much noise. When the host landed on the cold, hard slate in front of my knees, it sounded like a .45 going off in a broom closet. I froze. The old lady from Spain kneeling next to me looked like she might faint. Her husband crossed himself and said, *"Madre de Dios."* With two minutes left on the clock, I had fumbled Jesus.

God bless that palsied old priest. Without so much as skipping a beat, he reverently picked up the host, held it up to heaven, and murmured, *"Veni, veni, Sancte Spiritus,"* then closed his eyes and received it himself. He took another wafer from the Communion paten and waveringly placed it securely in the nest formed by my outstretched hands. Gazing deeply into my eyes, he said, "My son, this is the body of Christ."

What happened next is difficult to explain and perhaps, as with all mysteries, it is unwise to try. All I know is that in the moment of reception I was visited by God. Perhaps it was the goodness of the priest and his graciousness that silently opened a portal through which I momentarily made contact with the divine life. Or maybe it was the Eucharist itself—the host mingling with my brokenness, dissolving in saliva, coming to rest in the shallows of my heart's confusion. Kneeling at the altar, I was overwhelmed by the sense that my fragmented and discontinuous life might actually make sense.

In the blink of an eye, I moved from multi-verse to universe. The out-of-tune instruments that had played so cacophonously in my soul for so many years spontaneously came together and played one unmistakable chord with thundering clarity. Every grief, every joy, every loss, every hope, every disappointment—all the disparate pieces of my past, my present, and even my uncharted future—were instantly joined together, and I saw it all for what it really was. *Gift.* The gratitude I felt was nearly unbearable. I began to weep quietly, sobbing with release, rocking gently back and forth, holding the Communion rail to steady myself. I whispered over and over again the only prayer that really matters in this life: "Thank you, thank you, thank you."

How long did I remain there? I'm not sure. I only remember Kenny, Bernard, and Maggie coming around me like a painted triptych, hands resting gently on my shoulders, and the old palsied priest leaning over me and whispering in my ear, *"Grazie, Signore."*

✝ ✝ ✝

We arrived at the Leonardo da Vinci-Fiumicino Airport with only an hour to spare before the time to be at our gate. Kenny, Thomas, Bernard, and Peter waited as we checked our luggage. I stood in line and every so often glanced over my shoulder at them. I despaired of finding the right words to say good-bye. Leaving people is hard, especially when you've walked long miles together and you aren't sure when, or even if, you'll see them again. It occurred to me that the spiritual journey is so much about repeated departures. Abraham left Ur, Moses and the Isra-elites fled Egypt, the disciples dropped their nets and left their fathers, Jesus left the disciples and returned to the Father. Perhaps that's what Peter meant when he said that the pilgrimage is never over. Life on this side of the kingdom is a multi-leg journey, and sadly, this leg was over.

When our luggage was checked, Maggie handed me her backpack. "Can you hold this? I have to use the little girl's room," she said, not waiting for my answer.

"Hurry up," I called after her.

I walked slowly over to the guys who were waiting by the entrance to the security area. "Well, this is it," I said.

"So it is," Kenny said. The other three nodded.

"We have a gift for you," Peter said. He reached into his bag and pulled out a tau cross. Shaped like the nineteenth letter of the Greek alphabet and like a modern T, the tau cross is universally recognized as the symbol of the Franciscans. Francis had adopted it early in his ministry and signed most of his letters with it. The meaning of the symbol wasn't lost on the early Franciscans. They were to live cruciform lives, embracing the world in all its fallenness.

I gazed at the simple wood cross and cord in my hand. No gift had ever meant more to me. "I'll treasure this," I said quietly.

Kenny took it out of my hand and put it around my neck. He patted the cross on my chest. The four of us wrapped our arms around each other and formed a huddle, the crowns of our heads touching. The ground became blurry as I began to cry for the second time that day. At my feet, I saw the tears of my friends falling gently and mingling with my own.

"Do I get some of that?" Maggie had returned. We wiped our eyes and laughed. Bernard and Peter made room in the circle for Maggie to join us. Now we were complete.

After many more hugs and a prayer of blessing from Bernard, Maggie and I joined the long line of travelers waiting to pass through the metal detectors. The guys stood and waved at us until the very last moment. I picked up my bag from the conveyor belt and turned to look at them one last time. I peered into Kenny's eyes and silently formed the words, *Thank you.*

The Lord give you peace, he mouthed back. And with that, Maggie and I headed toward our gate.

XI

So you have failed? You cannot fail.

You have not failed; you have gained experience.

Forward!

SAINT JOSEMARÍA ESCRIVÁ

THE FLIGHT FROM ROME TO NEW YORK WAS A NIGHTMARE. WE stopped in Zurich, where a group of rugby players from Princeton boarded the plane. For eight solid hours, they celebrated their triumphant European tour with drinking games and bawdy songs sung at the top of their lungs. Maggie was impervious to the sophomoric hullabaloo and slept like a rock. I was exhausted but couldn't sleep. I was left with two options—watch *Sex and the City 2* or read *Sky* magazine. It's a good thing they don't allow sharp instruments on airplanes anymore, or I'd have slit my wrists.

By the time we got through customs and back to Thackeray, it was nearly three-thirty in the morning. There was no traffic on the streets, and a glaze of water from an earlier shower coated the road and shimmered under the streetlights. Maggie and I were lost in our own thoughts, feeling no compulsion to speak. I rolled down my window, and we listened to the tires skim over the wet asphalt. I pulled up in front of Maggie's apartment, popped the trunk, and carried her bags to her door.

Maggie fumbled to get her key in the door. "Can we talk tomorrow?" she asked.

"Sure, first thing," I said yawning.

Maggie turned and surprised me with a hug. "I had the time of my life," she said tearfully.

"I'm sorry your trip turned out to be so short. Maybe the next one will be on me," I replied.

✛ ✛ ✛

Homes act peevishly toward their owners after a long trip. When I walked in the door, mine acted like we'd never met before. It was miffed because I'd left in such a hurry and without so much as a good-bye. It was going to take a few days before it forgave me and warmed to having me back.

Before hitting the sack, I browsed through the mail. The day I left, I had asked my neighbor Jacqueline to forward to me in Italy anything that looked important and to leave the rest on my dining room table. All that remained was a two-foot pile of J.Crew catalogs and reams of credit card applications. Jacqueline had restocked my refrigerator and placed a note on the top shelf that read, "Welcome home!" I wondered if those two words would soon be mutually exclusive.

✛ ✛ ✛

The next morning, I awoke to someone relentlessly ringing my doorbell. Whoever it was had apparently decided they weren't leaving until they'd seen me. I fumbled around my bedside table looking for my alarm clock and discovered it was eleven o'clock. I stumbled out of bed and peeked through the curtains—Ed was standing on my doorstep, dressed like he was on his way to play tennis. Even though he'd been successful in business, Ed had never been totally accepted by Thackeray's more refined society, partly because of his lack of fashion sense. He was wearing a royal blue velour warm-up suit with bright-red piping on the sleeves and legs and an old pair of Stan Smith sneakers. He was a Walmart man in a Brooks Brothers world. I rummaged through the duffel on my bedroom floor to find a pair of jeans and T-shirt and ran to open the door.

"Welcome back," he said.

"Thanks," I said, haphazardly tucking in my shirt. "Come on in."

Ed leaned against the kitchen counter, arms folded, as I made coffee. I was heartbroken to see the watery brown liquid drip into the glass decanter. I resolved to buy a cappuccino maker, no matter how much it cost. *So much for my vow of poverty.*

I handed Ed a mug. "Want to sit outside?" I asked.

For some reason, the stoop in front of my condo was where Ed and I always talked, at least in warm weather. More key decisions about Putnam Hill had been made on those stairs than in my office.

"I thought I'd stop by to let you know what's happening," Ed said.

I had wondered what my first meeting with Ed would be like. Even though he'd sent me that conciliatory e-mail in Italy, I wasn't sure our friendship would ever be the same. It was too early to tell, but I thought I sensed a softening of his spirit toward me.

"You heard about the elders who resigned?" he asked.

"What was the final tally?"

"Three. Robinson, Carvin, and Whitehall."

I was sorry to hear about Carvin. He'd been one of our founding members. But I wasn't surprised, since none had been among the elders who came to my condo before I left for Italy. "Have they been replaced?" I asked.

"The church voted in Jim Lorne, Gary Miles, and Rod LeClerc to finish out the others' terms."

I frowned. "Aren't all three of those guys on the student ministries subcommittee?"

"Yep."

"Isn't that a little strange?" I asked, stating the obvious.

"Chip's developed quite a following who think he should replace you as senior pastor. When it came time to fill the vacant elder slots, they voted in people they knew would support him."

"And Chip?"

"He asked to meet with the elders after church yesterday," Ed said.

I sipped my coffee. "That's unusual. Why?"

"To tell us that if things didn't work out between you and Putnam Hill, he'd like to be considered for the job," he said.

I nearly choked. "That took some nerve."

Ed picked up a stray piece of gray stone and threw it onto the lawn. "Chip's a politician now, not a pastor," Ed replied. He didn't take to people who weren't straight shooters.

I put my coffee down on the stairs. "What should I do?" I asked.

Ed stood up and leaned against the handrail. "Where's your heart?"

Ed and I had swapped those two questions more times than I could remember. "It's in a good place, Ed. I'm clearer about things now than I've been in a long time," I answered.

"Got a vision for the church?" he asked.

"I worked on one in Italy."

Ed handed me a manila folder. "Someone else worked on one too."

I quickly scanned the document inside—a paper Chip had given to the elders describing where he'd take the church if he became senior pastor.

Ed looked at his watch and patted me on the shoulder. "Bring what you have to the meeting tonight," he said, standing and heading toward his car.

"Ed, I'm sorry about what happened," I called after him.

He turned and smiled. "Let's see if God comes out of the woods and shows himself."

I said a prayer of thanks as I watched him amble down my walk. The last time I'd seen him go down that path, I wasn't sure we'd ever talk again.

+ + +

The elders' meeting began at seven that night, and four hours later I was told I could leave. Several times during the session, I thought about those hearings they show on C-SPAN where some long-faced bureaucrat sitting in front of a microphone gets alternately praised or eaten alive by grandstanding senators.

When I walked out, Maggie was sitting on the floor in the hallway listening to her iPod. She tore out her earbuds and jumped up.

"How'd it go?"

"It was interesting," I said.

She slapped my arm. "That's all you're going to tell me?"

I smiled. "I apologized for everything that had happened and then told them about my time in Italy."

"And?" Maggie asked.

"Most of them were gracious. Then they asked me if I still felt called to be Putnam Hill's pastor."

"And?"

"I said yes—but that if I stayed, things would have to change. I passed around our document and went over it with them."

Maggie bit her lower lip. "What'd they say?"

"Miles and LeClerc said I'd lost my mind and demanded they vote right then and there on whether to fire me."

"Can they do that?" Maggie asked incredulously.

"The church bylaws say the elders are authorized to hire or dismiss pastoral staff. If Ed hadn't stepped in, it might have gone to a vote."

Throughout the meeting, Ed had been my champion. He'd barely said a word unless someone took a cheap shot at me, and then he had loudly cleared his throat and given them the "death stare." When LeClerc had tried to force a vote, Ed had spoken up like Moses himself standing on Mount Sinai and reading the tablets. He'd said I deserved better, and that the church would split if I weren't given the chance to present my ideas. There'd been some grumbling, but no one had dared to go nose to nose with a guy who used to eat the AFL–CIO for breakfast.

"So what's next?" Maggie asked.

"There'll be an all-church meeting after the morning service this Sunday," I said. "I'll get to share my vision for the church, and the church will tell the elders whether they want me back."

"No pressure," Maggie said.

"Yeah, right."

We walked out the front doors. I stopped halfway down the sidewalk and looked back at the church I'd spent so many years building. One hundred and twenty thousand square feet, a full-court gym, an education wing, an octagonal chapel connected to the thousand-seat auditorium by a glass breezeway—all framed by swaths of perfectly manicured lawns and a parking lot that was the envy of every pastor in town. Ground lighting shone up onto the facade of the building and the surrounding trees. It wasn't the Temple of Minerva, but it was still impressive.

"It's ironic," I said.

"What is?" Maggie asked.

"Chip's proposal is nearly identical to one I wrote five years ago. He played with the wording, added one or two unimaginative ideas, and told people he came up with it."

"In other words, he doesn't want to change a thing," Maggie said.

"Right. But the church deserves better. If he follows my old plan, it'll become a ghetto."

"But what if that's what the church wants?" Maggie asked.

"Then we need to try to talk them out of it," I said.

+ + +

The next few days were a flurry of activity. Maggie hadn't found a new job, so we spent most every day together. We did laundry, went to the grocery store, spent an afternoon shopping for a used car, and tried to find a smaller apartment for her.

Something had changed between Maggie and me, though neither of us dared to name it. When we said good-bye at the end of each day, I knew I was closer to being the man I wanted to be than I had been twelve hours earlier. Sometimes at the end of sentences, our eyes locked for a second longer than they used to, as though we were looking for confirmation that what was stirring in our hearts was real and mutual. One night after she left, I closed the door and laughed out loud. What on earth would my parents think if they knew I was falling for an ex-con? What would Maggie and my mother talk about when they met—needlepoint, and the fine art of making license plates?

Maybe all romances start with a healthy dose of incredulity.

On Friday I called Chip to ask if we could meet. Francis kept niggling me to be a peacemaker, and as awful as it felt, I knew I had to be the initiator. I left three voice mails and heard nothing back. On Saturday morning, I finally got an e-mail:

Chase,

I see no point in meeting with you. We've got different ideas about where the church should be going and it's up to the congregation to decide which direction it wants to take. I can only speak for myself, but I think it would be in the best interest of Putnam Hill for you to resign so the church can heal and move on. Apparently, the best interest of our church isn't as much a priority for you as it is for me.

> *Until Sunday,*
> *Chip*

Chip's patronizing tone was enough to send me over the edge. Maggie made me sit down at the kitchen table and recite the Serenity Prayer over and over until I stopped threatening to go burn his house down.

Saturday's mail brought news from Italy. Kenny wrote that Peter had finished his retreat and gone back to classes at the Sant'Anselmo in Rome. Bernard and Irene had headed off to a meeting in Malta, and Thomas hadn't been seen since Wednesday. Kenny had poked his head into his room, but there was no sign of him. Kenny was sorry they hadn't gotten a chance to say good-bye, but he wasn't surprised. Thomas was an enigma, and would remain so. Kenny ended his letter by saying that he was praying for me and wanted updates as events unfolded.

That night, Maggie came over and made lasagna al forno and surprised me with an Italian cheesecake she'd bought at a gourmet market. The label on the box had a pen and ink drawing of Mount Subasio on it. Just looking at it made me yearn to go back.

"Is this your version of the Last Supper?" I asked. I'd become increasingly anxious as the day wore on. One night back in Italy, Kenny and I had sat on the balcony at the friary while he told me that I was trying to complete the unfinished drama of my relationship with my father through my congregation. As the all-church meeting drew near, my neurotic insecurities began jumping up and down like angry monkeys screaming in a tree. Nothing so concentrates the mind as knowing that everything you've poured your life into for thirteen years is riding on one short presentation, and that the people you've cast in the role of your father might reject you. That'll disequilibrate the steadiest of minds.

Maggie got up to get the pecorino cheese in the fridge. "Who's preaching tomorrow?" she called from the kitchen.

"Chip is. The elders told me not to come until the service was over. They said my presence would distract people during worship." This request had been just one of several indignities I'd felt since returning home.

Maggie placed the bowl of cheese on the table and sat down. "What about the staff?" she asked.

"Mindy called," I said. Mindy was my director of pastoral care.

She was one of those people who lived for a good emergency. Whenever a member of the church had a crisis, Mindy would show up with a box of Kleenex and an industrial drum full of tuna casserole. She'd been one of my first and smartest hires.

"And?" Maggie asked.

"She said the staff was told not to call me, but she wanted me to know she was behind me. I asked her what the rest of the staff was feeling, and she said it was a mixed bag. She said if I left, lots of them would go at the same time," I answered.

Maggie shook her head. "What a mess," she said sadly.

For a few moments we ate in silence. Visions of what the all-church meeting would be like raced through my mind. The night before, I'd dreamed that the fourth-grade Sunday school class had morphed into a lynch mob and were chasing me around the sanctuary while the rest of the congregation sang "Blessed Assurance."

I stared down at my plate. "Maggie, I'm scared," I said.

She put down her fork and dabbed her mouth with her napkin. "You'd be a fool if you weren't," she said.

"I wish you could stand up and do the presentation with me."

First she looked surprised—and then the surprise melted into one of the most grateful expressions I'd ever seen. I wondered if Maggie would ever look as beautiful to me again as she did at that very moment. She gazed at me without speaking for a moment, then laughed. "An ex-con, recovering drug addict telling people how to do church? I don't think so." She laughed again, then sighed. "It means a lot to me that you even suggest it. But ... no. We've got to give this our best shot. I'll be there. Praying. But in the pew."

I nodded. "I guess you're right. But there's nobody who deserves to be up there more than you." Having Maggie stand beside me during the presentation would be great moral support —and professional suicide. Still—if Jesus or Francis were in my shoes, who would they ask to stand with them in the crucible?

Wouldn't it be a tarnished, limping lover of God like Maggie? Wouldn't they choose the foolish to teach the wise? It was lunacy, but there was also something poetic about it.

"Well," I said, "I'll do what I can. But after Sunday, I may be out of a job. I may be standing on a street corner wearing a cardboard sign: 'Will preach for food.'"

She laughed, then paused. "Well, one thing won't change." She pointed her fork at me. "Wherever you go, I'm going too."

Those six words jettisoned us across a border into a new and fearful land. Our fates were now intertwined.

✛ ✛ ✛

Chip's sermon that morning was titled "Church Next." He had the pulpit—and he used it to present his thoughts about where Putnam Hill should be heading. It came as no surprise that the proposal he'd given to the elders had by that time made its way into the hands of most everybody in the congregation.

The bylaws stated that only members were allowed to attend all-church meetings. After the morning service more than seven hundred of them stayed—an impressive turnout. When Maggie and I walked in, it felt like a scene from an old John Ford Western. I was the sheriff walking into Kitty's Saloon to confront the local bad guy. I knew, however, that a good number of people didn't think of me as the guy wearing the white hat. The crowds parted as we made our way down the aisle. A few people hugged me; others looked at the floor and shyly said hello. Some turned away and refused to say anything to me at all.

Ed met us at the front of the auditorium and shook my hand. "Ready?" he asked.

I nodded. Maggie and I took seats in the front row. Ed opened in prayer, then said, "On Monday night, the elders met with Chase and decided he should have the opportunity to talk about what he's learned over the last two months and share the direction he thinks our church should be moving. After he's done speaking, the elders will take questions, and then we'll ask for a show of hands to determine whether the church still has confidence in Chase's leadership. I should remind you, however, that the decision to keep or dismiss a senior pastor rests with the elders. We're only asking for a show of hands so we can know your opinions. Chase, I'll turn it over to you."

I walked up and faced the congregation, recalling what had happened the last time I stood there. The first person I saw was Dr. Mac, standing against the wall in the back of the room. He wasn't a member of the church, but he'd snuck in just as the meeting began. It was nice to know that my shrink was in the house. He would come in handy if I had a second psychotic episode. He smiled and gave me a thumbs-up.

I took a deep breath. "Years ago in Silesia, they built pulpits in the shape of a whale standing on its tail. In order to get to the dais, the pastor climbed a ladder through the whale's body until he emerged in the opening that represented its mouth, and from there he'd preach his sermon. The implication was that a pastor didn't have the right to preach until he'd spent some time wrestling with God, like Jonah did. Over the last two months, I've spent a lot of time in the whale's belly, and I hope that has given me the right to share with you the things that are on my heart. I'm trusting you won't spit me out on a beach when I'm done."

A few people chuckled, but the overall response wasn't reassuring. I was taking my clothes off one article at a time before a mostly unsympathetic room. Telling a nervous joke was something you did to distract your audience while you fiddled with a stuck zipper.

"I know the last time you all saw me, my personal stuff ended up causing many of you a lot of pain, and I'm truly sorry for that. I'm praying that God will use my mistakes to take Putnam Hill to a place we couldn't have gotten any other way."

I looked at Chip, sitting three rows from the front. He was trying to look impassive, but I knew he was nervous; this was a winner-take-all contest.

"I went on a pilgrimage—a spiritual journey—to find out what it meant to be a Christian, what it means to be the church, and to decide if I wanted to stay on that journey. In Italy, I found a mentor named Saint Francis of Assisi, who taught me that the church of the future needs to listen to the church of the past."

Bill Archer whistled quietly and snickered, while others turned and whispered to nodding neighbors. I could only imagine what they were saying. I felt prickly heat crawling up my neck.

"Look, I know Francis has been dead for eight hundred years, but try—"

"Saint Francis is Catholic," someone grumbled. It was Beatrice Connerly, one of the few elderly members we had at Putnam Hill. She was hard of hearing, and though I'm sure she thought her remark was barely audible, she might as well have used a bullhorn.

I swallowed hard and continued. "When I left here, I wasn't sure what a Christian looked like anymore. My idea of what it meant to follow Jesus had run out of gas. I started feeling less like a pastor and more like a salesman of a consumerized Jesus I didn't believe in. Learning about Francis helped me fall in love with Jesus again—and with the church again too."

I took another deep breath, looked at Maggie's shining face for affirmation, and held up my notes. "If nothing else, I want you to leave here this morning remembering five words: *transcendence*, *community*, *beauty*, *dignity*, and *meaning*. The kind of church I think can impact the world, and the type of church I want to lead, will be passionate about those ideals. This isn't a business plan, and it definitely won't be the next big trend in church growth," I said. "But if my journey taught me anything, it's that there aren't any simple formulas for being the church or following Christ—and anyone who tells you there are may be well-meaning, but they're out of touch with reality," I said, looking directly at Chip.

I put my notes on the podium, paused, and closed my eyes. This was it. I took a deep breath and looked up.

"The first word is *transcendence*," I said. "Since its beginning, Putnam Hill has tried to win people to faith principally by appealing to their intellects. Our assumption has been that the only true access to the soul is through the head, so our efforts to lead people to faith have focused on convincing their minds rather than captivating or romancing their hearts. From what I learned about the change Francis made in the church, he wouldn't have taken this approach. He was wary of scholars who wanted to talk about doctrines or abstract theological polemics in order to bring people to faith. He warned academics that knowing a lot *about* God could fool people into thinking they actually *knew* God, and there was a big, big difference between the two.

"Francis believed transcendent encounters with Jesus were the key to people's coming to faith. Opening our ears to God's voice in creation, being touched by the Spirit's presence in the community of believers, walking in solidarity with the poor, practicing contemplative prayer and meditation, saying the liturgy, and meeting Jesus in symbol-rich spaces and events like Communion —all of these are vital experiences that can act as portals into the life of God. If we want people to discover faith, we can't afford to ignore any of them. Francis understood this. He lived in an era when theology and knowledge were becoming the centerpieces of faith. Universities were being birthed across the known world. Scholars were organizing and codifying religious ideas into more rational systems of belief. But Francis cried out, 'Knowledge and theory are not sufficient! Encounter God! Encounter!' Just when the church was on the verge of collapse, that voice reawakened Europe's faith. We need to learn from him.

"All my life, I've been afraid to meet God anywhere else but in my head. Up here," I said, pointing to my temple, "I could keep God manageable and under control. But what kind of God can be controlled or managed? No God at all," I said, shaking my head.

"To create faith-producing moments, we need to reacquire some of the practices and attitudes Francis did. We also need to learn from other Christian traditions that emphasize different ways of encountering God, and integrate the best of their practices into the life of our church. No, we're not going to abandon theology," I said. "But the days when we could rely only on rational argument as the entry point to a relationship with God are fading fast."

The room was oddly quiet, as if there were an invisible membrane that separated me from the congregation. The unnatural hush was sucking me into the vortex of a full-blown panic attack. I shot a quick look at both Maggie and Mac and took a deep breath.

"The second word is *community*," I said. "Francis's vision of Christian community was pretty revolutionary for the times he lived in. He encouraged women to be in ministry and to follow his way of life. Women like Clare were his closest friends. He defied hundreds of years of church tradition by insisting members of his order live among the people instead of behind monastery walls. They didn't make artificial distinctions between the sacred and the secular. Instead, they went into the marketplace to minister. Francis and his other leaders saw their role as serving the members of the order rather than the other way around. As communities, they stood together against violence and injustice.

"The point I'm trying to make is that Francis focused on making his communities signs of the kingdom, the new Jerusalem. After spending a few weeks living with a bunch of Franciscans, I realized that we've been more about programs than about community here at Putnam Hill. We've been more of an organization, with me as the CEO, than an organism, an expression of Jesus on earth."

I looked up, saw the worry on Maggie's face, and knew I was in trouble. I'd been reading off my notes rather than interacting with the congregation. A seminar on the Death Tax Code would have been more scintillating. Those who weren't hostile were confused. I was losing them.

I took a deep breath, put my notes behind my back, and began to wing it. "OK, let's talk about what a genuine kingdom community looks like," I said. "First, if Francis were around today, he'd say our church community relies too much on words to tell others about our faith. For Francis, the gathered community was as potent a form of witness as words. He was convinced that how we live together is what attracts people to faith. Rather than loading people up with books and words when they come seeking God, why don't we just invite them into the community and say, 'We're all seeking God together—come join us. See how we relate to each other, to you, to the world. Experience God in our midst, and figure out if you want to be part of his family and what he's doing in the world.' It's all about actions first, words second."

A little better, but not much, I thought, watching the reactions on the faces before me. If Maggie had been up there with me, she at least would keep their attention. *And how would she do that?* I wondered. *What would she say about community? She'd push the envelope.*

"So, actions first, words second." I gulped. "Let's talk about our community and money."

You can always tell the natives from the transplants in New England. If you raise the subject of money, members of the old guard take on a very pained expression, as if you'd just put a container of used kitty litter under their noses. It's simply not good form to talk about m-o-n-e-y in Thackeray.

"Compared to the rest of the world, most of us are stunningly wealthy. What would someone who didn't go to church say if they drove by our parking lot on Sundays and saw the kinds of cars we drive—that we were on the consumerism gerbil wheel like everybody else? Things weren't much different in Francis's day. He faced having to do ministry in the same kind of materialistic environment that we do. Although the wealthy elite existed even before the time of Christ, conspicuous consumption was born in the thirteenth century. It was the first time in history that ordinary people had disposable income. Sadly, one of the most materialist institutions of all was the church. Regular people had a hard time taking Christianity seriously because the church had so much but shared so little. One of the reasons Francis inspired a revival across Europe was because he completely rejected consumerism and materialism. He'd got off the gerbil wheel. He gave up his wealth, which was considerable, and sometimes the shirt off his back to let others know that Jesus really was enough. Amazingly, his order was filled with aristocrats who followed his lead. Their sacrifice restored people's confidence in the gospel, and it shamed the institutional church.

"I'm not saying we should sell everything we have and give it to the poor. I'm saying that our materialistic society won't take us seriously as long as we're living with the same 'I shop; therefore I am' lifestyle.

"Francis taught me that if we spent less time worrying about how to share our faith with someone on an airplane and more time thinking about how to live radically generous lives, more people would start taking our message seriously. We'd have to make a new parking lot to handle the crowds who'd come to see the crazy rich folks who gave so much away to the poor. Radical? Maybe. But that's how the church's economy worked when the church first began." I was encouraged to see a few heads nodded approvingly.

"Over the last two years, we've raised five million dollars to beef up our endowment and build a new gym. It's funny, but Francis prohibited members of his order from touching money or having buildings. He was afraid it would lead to their getting too comfortable, too insulated from the world. I'm not saying money or buildings are all bad, but I'm wondering if at this point in our church's history, we're confusing preferences and need."

I looked over at Peter Collins, the kindly pediatrician who was also one of my elders. "Pete, remember the night we sat on your deck and you told me how you dreamed about starting an inner-city health clinic for the poor on the south side of Bridgewater?"

Looking surprised, Peter nodded.

"Given the choice between putting our money into a basket-ball court or a health clinic, which do you think Jesus would tell us to choose?" I asked.

Peter grinned.

"I need to repent of my collaborating with the powers of mate-rialism. I'm the worst of all sinners on that score. But if you take me back, I'm going to lead us all into a close examination of how we as a church are participating in the culture of consumerism. It won't be fun, but we need to think about whether our commu-nity's economics are aligned with the purposes of God's kingdom.

"Here's something else I learned — the kingdom commu-nity is a community of peacemakers. Francis told his friars to greet everyone they met by saying, 'The peace of the Lord be upon you,' which more often than not got them roughed up," I said, chuckling. "Thirteenth-century Europe was a violent place. There was always a war raging somewhere nearby, cities were filled with crime, disease killed people off right and left, and most of the roads were too dangerous to travel. The last thing people believed was that the Lord, or anybody else, could give them peace — and yet spreading peace is one of the most important ways a community can witness to the gospel."

I started to pace back and forth like a tiger in a cage, concen-trating with all my might on keeping my mind clear. I was push-ing hot buttons now, and I knew that some in the congregation would disagree violently with what I was about to say.

"The times we live in demand that we be more than peace lovers. The stakes are too high. As a community, we have to start being proactive peacemakers in our homes, our offices, our church—and, most importantly, in our world."

I shook my head. "Sometimes when I read Christian magazines or hear Christian leaders, it's downright scary. Liberals scream at conservatives, Republicans yell at Democrats, evangelicals berate revisionists, fundamentalists rail at everybody. It's like 'talk radio' Christianity—everyone believes they own the Truth and have a God-given mandate to shove it down others' throats. I admit it," I said, raising my hand, "I've even encouraged this kind of 'us versus them' spirit around here. I've even preached it, and I was wrong. Sure, we can disagree with others and sometimes we should—but whatever happened to gentleness and respect?"

I scratched my head and looked around. "When the church first began, it was a pacifistic movement known for its outspoken criticism of any form of bloodshed or violence. After Constantine legalized Christianity, 'just war' theory emerged, which meant that Christians could participate in wars if certain criteria were satisfied. By the year 1100, Christians were launching Crusades and telling the faithful that killing Muslims would secure them a spot in heaven! What happened? Somewhere along the way we forgot that Jesus intended the Sermon on the Mount to be an actual, concrete program for living. He wanted us to actually live it, not just admire it as a nice but unrealistic ideal. I mean, what would happen if Christians dedicated themselves to peacemaking with the same discipline and focus that armies do for war? What difference could it make? We have to revisit the early church's teachings about reconciliation, peacemaking, and the Sermon on the Mount and ask ourselves if we're living them out or tiptoeing around them."

The Marksteads and Dreisers stood up at the same time. Bill Markstead's face was purple, and his wife patted him on the back to keep him moving toward the exit. I think she was afraid he'd stand in the aisle and start a political debate with me if she didn't get him out. The Dreisers were in no such hurry. They made a few stops en route to the door to let their feelings be known. I saw their arms waving; a few times they gestured in my direction and shook their heads.

"One last point about being a community of peacemakers," I said. The Marksteads and the Dreisers paused at the doors to listen to me finish my thought. "I'm not a politician, and I'm not an expert on current affairs. But I learned in Italy that Christians are called to urge their leaders to be peacemakers too. This is one reason the church has to guard against holding up one political party as 'the Christian party.' History has proven that over-identifying with one party is a recipe for disaster. If we get too cozy with one group, we'll lose our ability to criticize them prophetically if they go off the rails."

The sound of the Marksteads and the Dreisers slamming the doors behind them made a few people jump.

Before the meeting, someone had opened the acoustic drapes. Shafts of noonday sun were shining down from near the ceiling line. The room was getting hotter, and I couldn't tell if the sweat on my forehead was a response to the rising temperature or a symptom of abject terror. I turned away from the congregation to wipe my forehead with my shirtsleeve.

"Francis's radical commitment to peace was another reason the church experienced a revival in Europe. I think it could have the same effect today. I'd like us to form a peace and reconciliation team to work with our missions committee to examine ways we can get involved in actively advancing peace locally and globally. How can we help combat unjust economic and political conditions around the world that create breeding grounds for violence and terrorism? Are there ways we can participate in reconciliation efforts between people groups in our country and abroad? How do we actively seek to apply Jesus' teachings in the Sermon on the Mount both here and globally?

"I wish I knew more about the arts," I said. "But I do know this: *Beauty* can break a heart and make it think about something more spiritual than the mindless routine we go through day after day to get by. Francis was a singer, a poet, an actor. He knew that the imagination was a stealth way into people's souls, a way to get all of us to think about God. For him, beauty was its own apologetic. That's why a church should care about the arts. They inspire all of us to think about the eternal.

"I wish I could have taken each one of you with me to Italy," I said, surprising myself when I realized I meant it. "I wish you could have experienced with me the way architecture and painting and sculpture and music all led me into the presence of God. I'm beginning to see that there's a difference between art that trusts beauty's simple power to point people to God and Christian art that's consciously propagandistic. My Uncle Kenny, with whom I spent most of my time in Italy, said something profound—that you can make art about the Light, or you can make art that shows what the Light reveals about the world. I think the latter is what we want to do. In a fallen world, beauty is a form of protest, a way to push back the darkness.

"Up to now, we've halfheartedly embraced the arts like they were nice but not necessary. I'd like to change that. What if we transformed our fellowship hall into a dedicated space for art exhibitions and live performances—built a stage in it for poetry readings, dance recitals, and plays? I want us to sponsor film series. Most of all, I'd like to create forums where we and our friends come to discuss the relationship between beauty, art, and faith and how all of it relates to our common search for God. We've been talking about hiring an associate pastor for evangelism, but I'd like us to consider hiring an 'artist in residence' instead. Let's give him or her freedom to make our church an outpost of beauty and to make Putnam Hill a safe place for artists to practice their vocations."

There was so much more to say about beauty. But my instincts told me to move on.

"Whenever I think of the word *dignity*, I think of Maggie Harmon. Most of us remember when Maggie first came to Putnam Hill, broken and hurting and with no idea how to act around us. And frankly, many of us had no idea how to behave around her either. But we made a place for her.

"Putnam Hill gave Maggie and Iris faith. But we gave Maggie something else besides—we helped give her her *dignity* back.

"We're all broken people who've lost our dignity, in one way or another. Francis's whole life was about giving people their dignity back—poor people, lepers, people who were despised and rejected by society—the very people Jesus sought out to minister to. His commitment to restoring people's sense of their God-given value thrilled the hearts of cynics who had all but given up on believing that the gospel was good news to anyone. What if we all, as a church, decided to make one of our distinctives being restorers of people's dignity? Make no mistake—this is indeed a radical and dangerous idea. It would mean we have to take people in just as they are, and coaxing their dignity back can take a long time. It would mean throwing open the doors of our church to folks who may be different from us. We might not always be comfortable with what they believe or how they live, but our job isn't to condemn people for their mistakes but to redeem them. Our goal is to help them see the One whose healing touch can bring back their lost dignity.

"Making dignity one of our guiding ideals would mean more than hospitality. Much more. It would mean fighting against anything that robs people of their dignity—things like racism, sexism, addictions, injustice, and poverty, to name a few. In last night's paper, I read that the drug and alcohol rehab in Robbins

Township just lost its lease. It's the only day program in the area for addicts who can't afford inpatient treatment. If it closes, 150 addicts will be left without the help they need to stay clean. Why don't we provide them temporary space in our building until they get a new facility? Again, this is just a start—but if we get going, God will tell us what to do next."

I became aware that my field of vision was filled with hundreds of eyes the size of dinner plates, staring at me in shock. Thank God for the handful of people sitting on the edge of their seats, looking like they were catching the vision.

"And here's a role for the church that will surprise you—one we've forgotten for far too long: we've got to give creation its dignity back too. If Francis were around today, he'd wonder why we weren't leading the charge to repair and defend our wounded planet. The earth is God's, and his people ought to stand up for it. Francis saw the stamp of God on everything. We can't fix everything, but maybe we can find an area in town that's trashed and make it beautiful for God again. We could adopt an endangered species and lobby the government for its protection. There are Christian organizations that are working to protect the environment—why not put them on our missions budget and send teams to work with them? That may not be much, but again, it's a start."

Seven or eight more people gathered their belongings and left. One man handed a note to LeClerc as he passed him. I was disappointed, but on the other hand, it could easily have been worse. "The last word is *meaning*," I said. "People are meaning-seekers. We all want to be part of something that's larger than ourselves. Our world is filled with people who have no big story that makes sense of their lives, and they're hungry for it."

I went back to my notes. "My Uncle Kenny made me read an author named Wendell Berry. Here's what he says: 'The significance—and ultimately the quality—of the work we do is determined by our understanding of the story in which we are taking part.' For years I thought of the Bible not as a story but as a black-and-white photograph, something you could use in a court of law to prove that our doctrines and propositions were rational and true. Talk about trivializing and holding back the beauty of the Bible! Now I see the Story more like a painting filled with glory, poetry, and even blurry lines. Paintings are trickier than photos. They're open to a wide variety of interpretation, depending on who's looking at them and the situations those viewers live in. Seeing the Bible this way could lead to things getting messy from time to time—but the Word is living, not static. Our job is to invite people to inhabit our story, to be part of what God's doing in history. And we don't need to feel constant pressure to defend it against its critics. Truth doesn't need defending. It is its own witness.

"So here's one last thing. The truth is, I don't want to be labeled an evangelical anymore. In fact I don't want to be labeled at all. Labels are misleading. They objectify people. They are a form of relational laziness. We think that if we can nail a person's label, we've got them all figured out and we don't need to spend time getting to know who they really are." I chuckled and shook my head. "People are always a lot more complicated than their labels."

I stopped and thought for a moment. "You know the story in the first chapter of John where Jesus is walking down the road, being followed by a couple disciples of John the Baptist? He turns to them and says, 'What do you want?' They say, 'Where are you staying?' Jesus replies, 'Come and see.'

"If someone insists on labeling me in the future, I'd like to be known as a 'come and see' Christian. If someone asks me what kind of church I belong to, I want to say, 'a come and see church.' Come and see how we love the poor; come and see how we give dignity back to those who've lost it or given it away; come and see how we encounter God through every practice at our disposal;

come and see how we love one another in community; come and see how we stand for peace and justice; come and see how we've been freed from consumerism and have become radically generous; come and see our passion for beauty; come and see how we defend the earth; come and see how we preach the gospel at all times and when necessary use words. Come and see—and perhaps after a while, you'll decide to join us in the story we're living in."

I sighed. "The Middle Ages were different from the world we live in now, but Francis faced a lot of the same challenges we do. I think he can help guide us to our goal, because his goal was the same as ours—*serving Jesus completely and unreservedly*. There's so much more to say about all of this. I don't have a five-year plan or strategy. All I've given you is a taste of the spirit of the church I want to lead. Now you'll have to figure out if that's the church you want to be."

The presentation had taken me about forty-five minutes. A few people clapped heartily; I saw some genuine enthusiasm on their faces. The rest gave an anemic round of polite golf applause. Ed got up from his seat and joined me in front, motioning to the rest of the elders. "I'll speak to you later," he whispered to me.

I headed down the center aisle. Maggie popped up and followed me. Halfway down the aisle, she grabbed my hand and squeezed it. I blanched when we hit the hallway outside the auditorium and she let out a war whoop.

XII

With God,
nothing is empty of meaning.
SAINT IRENAEUS

MAGGIE AND I WENT STRAIGHT TO THE CITY LIGHTS DINER TO
grab lunch to go. Some people lose their appetite when they're
nervous; some don't. The two of us were solidly in the "some
don't" camp. We bought enough food to feed a high school foot-
ball team coming off a two-week fast. We were sure Ed would
call as soon as he knew something, so we headed back to the
condo to wait. When the doorbell rang, I nearly tripped over an
ottoman rushing to get to it. I was surprised to see Mindy and her
husband, Jack, standing there. Mindy's eyes were red, and Jack
looked despondent.

"Have you heard from anyone yet?" she asked, sniffling.

Maggie came and stood behind me. "No," I said.

Mindy broke down and threw her arms around me. "I don't
think it looks good," she cried.

It was actually a blessing that Mindy was so upset, because
Maggie and I could focus on helping her deal with what had happened instead of having to deal with it ourselves. Maggie made
coffee, and we sat around the kitchen table and listened to the
blow-by-blow from Jack and Mindy.

"After you left, the meeting turned into a free-for-all. Some
people thought your ideas were great and said the church owed it
to you to try them out. But there was a bigger group that said you
had turned into a left-wing liberal Catholic, and a womanizer to

boot." Mindy looked apologetically at Maggie. "A few said they weren't even sure you were still a Christian," she said, blowing her nose.

"Then what happened?" I asked.

"Ed told everyone that the elders valued their input and asked them to pray that God would give the church's leadership wisdom about what to do next," Jack said. "Then the elders left and went to your office to meet. I bet they'll make a decision before tomorrow."

"And Chip?" Maggie asked.

Mindy scowled. "He didn't say a word—just sat there looking smug and self-satisfied."

There was a knock on the door and the sound of a familiar voice calling hello. When I came round the corner into the living room, Ed was standing there. He threw his hat on the couch. "Got time to talk?" he asked.

+ + +

Mindy and Jack didn't say much to Ed on the way out. I walked them to the front door, while Maggie went to the kitchen and closed the door behind her. I could hear her scrubbing pots and pans that I knew weren't dirty. Ed sat on the couch, and I took the chair across from him.

"The elders voted to let you go," he said.

My shoulders collapsed. I should have been less surprised. I thought I'd prepared myself for it. But actually hearing the words was devastating. "What happened?" I asked.

"It was a close call. We were deadlocked at four to four for three hours," he said.

"Who changed his vote?" I was sure it must have been Roger Pernall. He was always the most easily swayed.

Ed leaned forward. "I did," he said, looking directly into my eyes.

My heart went into a free fall inside my chest; for a moment, I couldn't get air into my lungs. In my mind, I saw the two of us fifteen years earlier, playing golf and talking about my dream for a new church. Even though I was thirty years his junior and a little full of myself, he'd taken the time to listen and ask all the hard questions. After nine holes, he'd said my ideas were exciting. By the eighteenth hole, he was my founding elder.

"But why?" I asked.

Ed sighed. "If you stayed here, this church would whittle you down to nothing. You'd spend the next five years arm-twisting committees and naysayers to follow your lead. You'd die from a thousand small cuts."

"This was a mercy killing?"

"Pretty much."

I'd once heard someone define denial as "refusing to know what you already know." In my heart of hearts, I'd known all along that it would be easier to push an elephant through a garden hose than to change Putnam Hill. At the same time, I had refused to know it. Ed had seen it clear as day. He'd done the right thing.

I rubbed my eyes. "Any advice?" I asked.

"Start over," he said.

EPILOGUE

Let us begin again,
for up to now we have done nothing.
SAINT FRANCIS, *in the last days of his life*

Journal Entry:
June 17

It's been a long time since I felt the way I did earlier tonight. I put out the word that I was having a gathering at my condo to talk about starting a new church, and forty people showed up! Two-thirds were laypeople and soon-to-be-former staff from Putnam Hill who were intrigued by what they'd heard at the all-church meeting, and the rest were interested friends (even my neighbor Jacqueline showed up).

It was just like the old days when I started Putnam Hill. Maggie and I made a huge bowl of fettuccine primavera (in honor of Francis), and a few other people brought dessert, salad, and bread. I was just beginning to share my vision with the group when Ed walked in, with Mac right behind him. I was so moved I almost couldn't finish my talk. Ed half sat on a windowsill in the back of the room and grinned like a Cheshire cat the whole time. I made a mental note that the two of us needed to play golf again. I was psyched to see Mac too. The fact that I'm even entertaining the idea of planting a new church is an indication that I need a full-time shrink around. At the end of the evening's program, we celebrated Communion together. It was very powerful. Ed came forward and served beside me, while Mindy passed out Kleenex.

I got word that Putnam Hill has formed a search committee to find a new pastor. Chip's serving as interim and will probably end up getting the job. Truth is, I wish the church well. I love them dearly, and I've promised myself that every time I drive by it, I'll send up a prayer.

We don't have a name for the new church, nor do we have much money, but there's plenty of passion to go around. Maggie's agreed to work as my part-time secretary, which should be interesting since she has virtually no organizational skills. I'm not sure where she and I are heading, but I do know that she grows on me more and more every day. She says we have to take it "one day at a time," and I think that's wisdom.

Last night, the two of us were sitting on the couch, and Maggie suddenly realized where she'd seen Umberto before. He was the guy who told her to come to Italy in her dream. I'm not sure what to make of that, and I probably shouldn't try. Suffice it to say, maybe Carla was right. Some people live with such a ferocious intensity and beauty that their spirit never quite leaves this world.

I found my old copy of Dante's Divine Comedy under my bed earlier today. It must have fallen out of my duffel when I was unpacking. I opened it to the last page and saw that long ago I had circled the closing lines of the Inferno.

> By that hidden way
> My guide and I did enter, to return
> To the fair world: and heedless of repose
> We climbed, he first, I following his steps,
> Till on our view the beautiful lights of heav'n
> Dawn'd through a circular opening in the cave:
> Thus issuing we again beheld the stars.

Indeed.

FURTHER REFLECTIONS
FOR THE PILGRIM'S JOURNEY

CHASING FRANCIS IS WRITTEN IN A GENRE CALLED WISDOM LIT-
erature, which is a delicate balance of fiction and nonfiction, pilgrimage and teaching. Halfway through the book I realized I
couldn't include everything I wanted to say about Francis and the
church without having the story grind to a complete halt under
the weight of too much historical and theological exposition. I
ended up cutting a lot of material and creating a study guide for
people who want to explore more deeply some of the topics raised
in the story. If you want to get the most out of this book, I urge
you to read this guide — either alone or, preferably, in a discussion group.

I

Saint Francis went through a spiritual crisis, a "dark night of the
soul," just before the awakening of his faith. In *The Road to Assisi*,
Paul Sabatier writes:

> The miserable emptiness of his life suddenly appeared
> before him; he was terrified at his solitude, the solitude of a
> great soul in which there is no altar.
>
> Memories of the past assailed him with intolerable bitter-
> ness. Seized with a disgust of himself, he found that his for-
> mer ambitions seemed to him ridiculous or despicable. Francis
> went home overwhelmed with the weight of a new suffering.

In such hours of moral anguish we seek a refuge either in
love or in faith. By a holy violence he was to arrive at last at a
pure and virile faith, but the road to this point was long and
sown thick with obstacles, and at the moment at which we
have arrived he had not yet entered upon it; he did not even
suspect its existence. All he knew was that pleasure leads to
nothingness, to satiety and self-contempt.

PAUL SABATIER, *The Road to Assisi*, p. 10

In chapter 1, Chase experiences a crisis of faith. In Chase's case,
his traditional evangelical spirituality no longer seems to satisfy his
thirst for God. In addition, he's fed up with the baggage that fre-
quently goes along with the Christian subculture — its music, literature, language, and insularism; a packaged or "McDonaldized"
approach to spiritual growth that promises more than it delivers;
the cult of Christian celebrity; and a spirit of theological and political triumphalism, to name a few. Perhaps Chase is unwittingly
becoming what Dave Tomlinson calls a "post-evangelical":

Most people who contemplate the possibilities of being
"post"-evangelical do so because of the difficulty they have
reconciling what they see and experience in evangelicalism with their own values, theological reflection, and intuition. For some people the agony created by this conflict is
considerable.

For example, one young man, who had grown up in an
evangelical home, spoke to me of the pain of his dilemma: "I
don't know where to go. I no longer feel I can call myself an
evangelical, yet I certainly don't wish to be a liberal. What
am I?" Others are more nonchalant about it, like the young
woman who said, "Evangelicalism helped me to begin with,
but I feel I've outgrown it now." Arrogant? Possibly. Yet she
voiced something that cropped up continually in my discussions with people — the feeling that while evangelicalism is

supremely good at introducing people to faith in Christ, it's distinctly unhelpful when it comes to encouraging a more "grown up" experience of faith.

DAVE TOMLINSON, *The Post-Evangelical*, p. 24

1. Respond to this statement: "I love Jesus—it's Christianity that drives me crazy."

2. Dave Tomlinson writes, "To be post-evangelical is to take as given many of the assumptions of evangelical faith, while at the same time moving beyond its perceived limitations" (p. 28). Have you found that the culture or theology of evangelicalism suffers from any limitations? If so, describe and discuss them.

3. Have you ever experienced a crisis of faith or an event that made you question what you believed? If so, are you willing to discuss it?

4. How would you counsel someone who has become cynical about or disillusioned with the culture or theology in their church? Have you ever felt this way? If so, what was it like?

5. Longtime Christians often feel afraid to voice their unease with the "certainty and absoluteness of much evangelical theology" (Tomlinson, p. 30). How can we make church a place where *everyone* can feel safe to voice doubts and struggles and still feel valued and accepted?

II

A friend of mine describes the Bible as a travelogue. It's a sacred book filled with *pilgrims*—people who felt called out on a spiritual journey because of an inner ache, yearning, or "voice" they couldn't quiet. Their journeys were filled with detours, disobedience, roadblocks, and rich encounters with the merciful triune God.

In their book *The Journey: A Guide for the Modern Pilgrim*, Michael and Maria Ruiz Scaperlanda describe the sacred pilgrimage as "the journey of those who deliberately seek answers to the questions of meaning, purpose, and eternity. Instead of seeking fulfillment in things that will never satisfy, the sacred pilgrim sets out to find that which the heart truly desires: God's very presence" (p. 10).

1. Traditionally, pilgrimages have been understood as physical journeys that mirror and energize an inner spiritual journey. Have you ever intentionally made a physical journey somewhere as a way of marking your inner spiritual journey? If so, share your experience. If you could design a pilgrimage what would it be like? Where would you go? What would you do?

2. Chase's Uncle Kenny implies that there is a big difference between people on the spiritual journey who are pilgrims and those who are merely tourists. Play with that metaphor. What do you think some of the differences are between a spiritual pilgrim and spiritual tourist?

3. Have you ever thought of your journey with Christ as a pilgrimage? What does intentionally looking for "answers to the questions of meaning, purpose, and eternity" look like? Does this search end once one comes to faith?

4. Spend a few minutes talking about your spiritual pilgrimage. Describe the terrain you've passed through so far. What are some of the roadblocks and detours you've experienced? Where are you now?

5. Thomas Merton said he was drawn to sacred sites, not because he knew the places, but because he believed the places knew him. Have you ever visited a "shrine" or holy place and experienced a heightened awareness of God's presence? Do you have a "sacred site" where God is more real to you than anywhere else?

6. Duane W.H. Arnold and C. George Fry relate an episode from the life of famed twentieth-century pilgrim William McElwee Miller:

> While traveling along the border of Iran and Afghanistan, Dr. Miller had encountered a Muslim sage. Together the missionary and the mullah rode along the narrow path. In the course of their conversation the Persian asked the Presbyterian, "What is Christianity?" Dr. Miller said, "It is like a journey. For that trip I need four things — bread, for nourishment; water, for refreshment; a book, for direction; and opportunity, for service. These are my pilgrim fare. Jesus provides me with these things. I trust him on my way. That is Christianity.
>
> DUANE W.H. ARNOLD AND C. GEORGE FRY,
> *Francis: A Call to Conversion*, p. 79

How would you interpret Miller's answer? How would you answer someone who asked you to define Christianity if you could only use metaphors to answer? What kinds of practices nourish your spiritual pilgrimage?

III

In Chase's first journal entry, he writes about feeling like a character who doesn't know his Author anymore. For Chase, simply having sound doctrine and theology isn't enough to sustain his faith any longer. The cry of his heart is, *"Is this all there is? There has to be more to following Jesus than this!"* Uncle Kenny suggests this might be because Chase's understanding of the Bible is distorted. For most of his Christian life, Chase viewed the Scriptures as a perfectly strung-together history of ideas designed to support doctrines, rather than the messy "story of how God gets back what was always his in the first place."

Kenny believes that Chase (as well as other people living in a postmodern world) is hungry for a more "storied faith" — an awareness that they are participating in a larger cosmic drama or narrative, called the gospel.

In his book *The Great Giveaway*, David Fitch writes:

> Let us then move beyond seeing Scripture as a collection of truth propositions that need to be scientifically dissected, inductively sliced, and distributed to Cartesian, rational selves sitting in the pews. Instead, let us come to Scripture as the grand narrative of God in Jesus Christ where God has revealed himself down through the ages from Abraham to Moses, the nation of Israel to the ultimate person and work of Jesus Christ. It is real history, but let us not make it into scientific history where we know it only as distanced selves dissecting an object. Rather it is the narrative of God into which we have been invited to participate. It is alive and it discloses the world where Jesus is Lord, and God is at work through Jesus Christ to save the world ... Amidst the carnival of narratives that society has become, let us come to worship under his grand story to be engulfed by it so as to live it out in contrast to the world's stories.
>
> DAVID FITCH, *The Great Giveaway*, pp. 141–42

1. **Review Kenny and Chase's conversation in the Brancacci Chapel. For you, has the Bible been more of a painting (grand story) or a black-and-white photograph (a history**

of ideas that can be scientifically dissected or inductively sliced)?

2. The culture offers people a "carnival of narratives" to choose from that seek to explain the way the world is. What are some of the more popular alternatives to the grand story articulated in the Bible?

3. In an essay titled "Christianity and the Survival of Creation" from *Sex, Economy, Freedom, and Community*, Wendell Berry writes that "the significance—and ultimately the quality—of the work we do is determined by our understanding of the story in which we are taking part." How do you understand the "grand story" of God in which you are taking part? How does knowing your story determine the significance and quality of the way you work and live?

4. Kenny argues that "no one tradition has a corner on the faith market. Sharing the wisdom each of our traditions brings to the table will create more well-rounded Christians. Francis was a Catholic, an evangelical street preacher, a radical social activist, a contemplative who devoted hours to prayer, a mystic who had direct encounters with God, and someone who worshiped with all the enthusiasm and spontaneity of a Pentecostal. He was a wonderful integration of many of the theological streams we have today." Do you agree that each denominational expression of the body of Christ has unique practices and wisdom we all can learn from? What are some of the "best practices" from other Christian traditions that you could integrate into your own?

IV

Many people today would laugh if you said the church in North America needed repairing. They might reply, "The church isn't falling down today. Megachurches are springing up like weeds. Christians have more political clout and cultural visibility than ever. Christian authors sell tens of millions of books and produce movies that generate hundreds of millions of dollars in revenue. These are the glory days!"

Strangely enough, when Jesus spoke to Francis from the crucifix at the Chapel at San Damiano, the church was at the zenith of social and political power. It was the world's largest investment banking firm. The arts, philosophy, architecture, literature, and music all issued forth from the church. Jesus, however, wasn't fooled by the medieval church's outward appearance of success. Jesus said, "Francis, go and repair my house. You see it is falling down."

1. In spite of the fact that some segments of the church today are experiencing "success," do you think it still needs repairing? If yes, where do you believe it's broken?

2. What are some of the "stones" we'll need to use in repairing the twenty-first-century church? For example, the stone of a new radical generosity, the stone of the arts, the stone of embracing versus excluding, the stone of community, etc. What stone has God specifically given you to contribute to the effort?

3. Father Romano Guardini once said, "The church is the cross on which Christ is always crucified." What do you think that means? Is it true?

4. Before God could use Francis to rebuild the church, he had to rebuild Francis. How is God rebuilding you right now?

V

Thomas of Celano writes these words about Saint Francis:

> When he found an abundance of flowers, he preached to them and invited them to praise the Lord as though they were endowed with reason. In the same way he exhorted with the sincerest purity cornfields and vineyards, stones and forests and all the beautiful things of the fields, fountains of water and the green things of the gardens, earth and fire, air and wind, to love God and serve him willingly. Finally, he called all creatures brother, and in a most extraordinary manner, a manner never experienced by others, he discerned the hidden things of nature with his sensitive heart, as one who had already escaped into the freedom of the glory of the sons of God. O good Jesus, he is now praising you as admirable in heaven with all the angels, he who on earth preached you as lovable to every creature.
>
> THOMAS OF CELANO, *St. Francis of Assisi*, pp. 72–73

Theologian Martin Buber made a distinction between the two fundamental ways people encounter and relate to reality. He defined them as the "I-It" and the "I-Thou" relationships. We typically treat physical objects and animals in an impersonal "I-It" manner and reserve the "I-Thou" relationship for people—knowing that they, like us, bear the sacred image of God. As you can see in the quotation above, Francis related to the world in a revolutionary manner. For him, there was no such thing as an "I-It" relationship. He honored everything in creation, the animate and inanimate, by interacting with them in an "I-Thou" manner.

In his essay titled "Christianity and the Survival of Creation," Wendell Berry writes:

> We will discover that, for these reasons, our destruction of nature is not just bad stewardship, or stupid economics, or

a betrayal of family responsibility; it is the most horrid blasphemy. It is flinging God's gifts into his face, as if of no worth beyond that assigned to them by our destruction of them. To Dante, "despising Nature and her gifts" was a violence against God. We have no entitlement from the Bible to exterminate or permanently destroy or hold in contempt anything on the earth or in the heavens above it or in the waters beneath it. We have the right to use the gifts of Nature, but not to ruin or waste them. We have the right to use what we need, but no more, which is why the Bible forbids usury and great accumulations of property.

WENDELL BERRY, "Christianity and the Survival of Creation," in *Sex, Economy, Freedom, and Community*, p. 308

Later in the same essay Berry writes, "We are holy creatures living among other holy creatures in a world that is holy. Some people know this, and some do not. Nobody, of course, knows it all the time. But what keeps it from being far better known than it is? Why is it apparently unknown to millions of professed students of the Bible? How can modern Christianity have so solemnly folded its hands while so much of the work of God was and is being destroyed?" (pp. 308–9).

Francis was more than just a nature mystic. It can be argued that he was the first environmental activist. Adrian House writes about Francis's intervening with political authorities and serving as an advocate for God's creatures: "He once said, 'If I ever talk to the emperor I will implore him, for the love of God, to decree that no one should trap or in any way harm our sisters the larks. Likewise, the lord of every town and village, and every *podestà*, should see that all their people scatter the road with grains for the birds on Christmas Day'" (Adrian House, *Francis of Assisi: A Revolutionary Life*, 250).

In *The Little Flowers of St. Francis*, we find another story that shows his willingness to intercede on behalf of creatures:

A boy of the town of Siena caught a number of turtle doves in a snare, and he was carrying them all alive to the market to sell them.

But St. Francis, who was always very kind and wonderfully compassionate, especially toward gentle animals and little birds, was stirred by love and pity on seeing the doves. And he said to the boy who was carrying the doves: "Good boy, please give me those doves so that such innocent birds, which in Holy Scripture are symbols of pure, humble, and faithful souls, will not fall into the hands of cruel men who will kill them."

The boy was then inspired by God to give all the doves to St. Francis.

When the kind Father had gathered them to his bosom, he began to talk to them in a very gentle way, saying: "My simple, chaste, and innocent Sister Doves, why did you let yourselves be caught? I want to rescue you from death and make nests for you where you can lay your eggs and fulfill the Creator's commandment to multiply."

And St. Francis took them with him and made a nest for all of them.

RAPHAEL BROWN, *The Little*
Flowers of St. Francis, p. 91

1. What do you think of Francis's unusual way of relating to everything in God's creation in an "I-Thou" relationship? Describe how you relate to the environment and how it factors in to your spiritual life. How would it change you if you began to live more aligned with Francis's vision of the created order?

2. Do you agree with Berry's assertion that the destruction or exploitation of the environment is as an act of blasphemy?

Ian Morgan Cron

3. Some would say that most Christians have silently stood by while others actively despoiled and destroyed vast portions of the earth. Do you think this is true? If so, why do you think we have behaved in this way?

4. Respond to this statement: "We can no more say we love the Creator and then ignore the maltreatment of his creation than we can say we love an artist but despise their paintings."

5. Read Genesis 1:26–31; Psalm 19:1–5; Psalm 24:1–2; John 1:1–3; Romans 8:22–24; and Colossians 1:15–20. Taken together, how might these passages begin to inform and shape your understanding of the Christian's responsibility to steward creation?

6. Should the church become more committed to creation care? Discuss practical strategies for how you and your church could defend God's creation against further abuse and exploitation.

VI

In *Francis of Assisi: A Revolutionary Life*, Adrian House writes:

Our reliance on symbols, icons, rituals, and sacraments, at the key moments of social, ceremonial and religious occasions, manifests a primal need to express our most potent desires or aspirations through familiar objects and gestures. Vice versa these—a loving cup, raised banners, the lowered sword, a gold ring, the scent of smoke or proffered bread and wine in the Mass—stimulate our senses and through them our minds, imaginations, and emotions. These, in turn, activate our wills and stir us to action.

ADRIAN HOUSE, *Francis of Assisi: A Revolutionary Life*, p. 253

Human beings are incurable symbol makers. We are creatures who love ceremony (and sometimes even pageantry) to mark moments and life passages that we recognize as significant (for example, weddings, funerals, graduations). As Adrian House points out, one of the effects and purposes of symbols, ceremonies, and sacraments in the church is to awaken our wills and to move us to action.

In *The Younger Evangelicals*, Robert Webber reminds us that, for the first fifteen hundred years of church history, the Eucharist was the primary means by which people encountered or experienced God. It was only after the Reformation that the locus of God's presence was transferred to the Word. The assertion is that we threw the baby out with the bathwater. Maybe Francis got it right:

> Francis recognized and restored the centrality of the Eucharist, saving worship from two imbalances that have existed in both Catholic and Protestant Christianity. The first imbalance is the elevation of the pulpit at the expense of the altar, so that instead of being "friends," Christians are reduced to being "students" and the church becomes a school with a professor-student relationship rather than a family. This was an abuse common to some of the friars and preaching orders in the medieval church and of an extreme Protestantism in the modern church, epitomized by a sanctuary with no altar, only a central pulpit. The second imbalance is the separation of the altar from the people so that they become "spectators," viewing the eucharistic liturgy rather than participating in Communion. This is a danger found in some medieval forms of Catholic Christianity and is evident in certain segments of Protestantism today.
>
> DUANE W.H. ARNOLD AND C. GEORGE FRY,
> *Francis: A Call to Conversion*, p. 73

1. In many churches there is a new level of appreciation for the liturgy and Eucharist. Why do you suppose that is?

2. Chase came to appreciate the liturgy for how it connected him to all Christians who came before him and how it helped relocate him inside the redemption story. Have you ever worshiped in a church that used a liturgy? What was it like for you?

3. It has been said that one reason for repeatedly performing the liturgy is so that it insinuates itself so deeply into your bones that you eventually *become* the liturgy. What do you think of that idea? What might it mean to "become the liturgy"?

4. Francis's ministry was grounded in the sacramental and liturgical life. It was the wellspring of his soul. Gerard Straub writes:

> Saint Francis of Assisi experienced the Eucharist as a Sacrament of Love in which God became his spiritual food. He needed the refreshment of Love's presence the way his lungs needed air. Nourished by Love, Francis was able to love in turn all of creation. As Christ's Body and Blood became one with Francis' body and blood, Francis was able to become Christ to everyone he met.
>
> GERARD STRAUB, *The Sun & Moon Over Assisi*, p. 267

Have you ever thought of the Eucharist this way? How would you explain the sacraments to someone who had never been to church? What's the wellspring of your soul?

5. This chapter also considers the vital impact of sacred space on the worshiper and the worship experience. In his wonderful little book titled *Heaven in Stone and Glass*, Catholic theologian Father Robert Barron writes:

One of the serious problems that we face is that for the past thirty years this iconic element has been undervalued. Our church buildings have become largely empty spaces, void of imagery and color, places where the people gather but not places that, themselves, tell a story ... St. Augustine said that the mind delights in a truth that comes in an indirect and symbolically evocative way. The cathedrals teach the truth of Christ in precisely this delightfully indirect manner.

ROBERT BARRON, *Heaven in Stone*
and Glass: Experiencing the Spirituality
of the Great Cathedrals, pp. 12–13

Chase learns that sacred space can help evoke a divine encounter. In some mysterious way, the architecture speaks and teaches us about God through windows, towers, symbols, vaults, naves, altars, lighting, and smells of incense. Have you ever been inside a cathedral or worshiped in one? Describe the experience. How was your experience of the Great Mystery, the transcendent God, enhanced by the architecture and sense of sacred space?

6. Building cathedrals today would be prohibitively expensive. Suppose your church meets in a warehouse, living room, or school auditorium. How might you exercise your "medieval imagination" and create a sacred space for worship? What modern media can you use to create a sacred environment that evokes awe, reverence, and a sense of God's majesty? How might you create a sacred space in your home where you can meet and worship God alone?

7. If you could design the ideal church, with money being no object, what would it look like?

VII

As you read the quotations found within the next several questions, consider the implications for our attitude as Christians toward beauty and the arts.

1. William Blake writes, "A Poet, a Painter, a Musician, an Architect—the Man or Woman who is not one of these is not a Christian."

   What on earth is Blake trying to say? Is he right?

2. In a message delivered in 2005 at Trinity Church in Greenwich, Connecticut, celebrated artist Makoto Fujimura remarked, "The arts, especially the visual arts, and the church have had a strained relationship in recent times. Many view artists with suspicion today. In many congregations, very little attention is paid to visual materials. On the other hand, artists are often furious at the institution of the church, often resorting to denigrating the sacred to create shock, often drawing attention to their personal pains of experiencing alienation, or, worse yet, abuse within houses of worship."

   Why do you think there's been a strained relationship between artists and the church? Should the arts be more important to Christians and churches than they are today? Why, or why not? Is your church the kind of community where painters, dancers, filmmakers, poets, writers, sculptors, and actors would be welcome and celebrated for their unique contribution to the advancement of the kingdom, or would they feel misunderstood or alienated? How might the church better integrate the arts and artists into its life?

3. Consider the following account from the life of Saint Francis, as well as the excerpt from David Mill's article "Imaginative Orthodoxy."

Francis composed a melody to go with the words of his poem, and sent some of the brothers to various places in order that in singing it they would convey its profound truth to their listeners. He instructed them in how to do this: like traveling medieval minstrels who sang of brave knights and their true loves, they were to form a circle in marketplaces and town squares, wherever people gathered. One of their number was to preach a sermon, and immediately afterward all of them were to sing Francis' Canticle of Brother Sun. The one who had preached was then to turn to the people and say, "We are the wandering minstrels of God and the only reward we ask is that you lead a life of true penitence."

In response to the brothers' surprise at thus being called "itinerant minstrels," Francis asked: "Who indeed are God's servants, if not minstrels who seek to move men's hearts in order to lead them into the joys of the spirit?"

PAUL M. ALLEN AND JOAN deRIS ALLEN, *Francis of Assisi's* Canticle of the Creatures: *A Modern Spiritual Path*

The artist's job is to reveal the real nature of things through picture or story or song, to show the rest of us what is really there when we are content with the misleading surface of things. As Pope John Paul II has written, "Artists are constantly in search of the hidden meaning of things, and their torment is to succeed in expressing the world of the ineffable." Through their work, in the words of the Vatican II document *Gaudium et Spes*, "the knowledge of God can be better revealed and the preaching of the Gospel can become clearer to the human mind."

DAVID MILLS, "Imaginative Orthodoxy: The Art of Telling the Christian Story," *Touchstone*

Both Saint Francis and Pope John Paul II believed that few media witness to the truth and beauty of the gospel

quite like poetry, song, dance, story, the visual arts, film, and theater. Has that been your experience? Explain the impact.

4. When have you richly encountered God in a gallery, book, performance, or film? Try to explain what happened to you and why.

5. Imagine two artists. Both are Christians. One creates works of art that do not consciously or overtly attempt to present a Christian view of the world. The other artist creates works that are blatantly Christian and intends them to be used for evangelistic purposes. Is one work less spiritual than the other?

6. In this chapter in *Chasing Francis*, over dinner with Chase and Carla, Liam says, "The church is realizing there is an awareness of God sleeping in the basement of the postmodern imagination and they have to awaken it. The arts can do this. All beauty is subversive; it flies under the radar of people's critical filters and points them to God. As a friend of mine says, 'When the front door of the intellect is shut, the back door of the imagination is open.' Our neglect of the power of beauty and the arts helps explain why so many people have lost interest in church. Our coming back to the arts will help renew that interest."

   Chase's Uncle Kenny claims that in addition to scholar-pastors, the church will need more artist-pastors in the postmodern era. Do you think he's right? Why, or why not? How would they be different from each other?

7. Imagine you were hired to launch an arts program at your church and were given a blank check to do it. What kinds of things would you do?

VIII

Francis's commitment to the ministry of peacemaking and reconciliation can't be overemphasized. It was a hallmark of his movement. Members of his order were forbidden from carrying arms or
from shedding blood under any circumstances. There are numer-
ous examples of his stepping in to broker peace between warring
families, between cities, even between people and animals. Of
the many stories that we have, few are as famous (or as relevant
to the world we live in today) as the account of Francis's attempt
to secure a peace agreement between Christians and Muslims to
end the Crusades.

In 1219, Francis and his companion Illuminatus went to the
port city of Damietta in Egypt where the Crusaders had been
holding the fortress of the Sultan Al-Kamil under siege for more
than a year. When they got there, they were appalled by the sav-
agery of the Christian and Muslim armies. Christian soldiers were
involved in rapes, looting, killing women and children—all under
a banner bearing the cross of Christ. For a few days, Francis and
Illuminatus tried preaching repentance and reconciliation among
the Crusaders, and when this didn't stop the killing, Francis went
to the head of the armies, Cardinal Pelagius, and begged him to
accept the sultan's generous peace terms.

The cardinal was dead set on crushing the Muslims, so Francis
decided to take matters into his own hands and make a personal
visit to the sultan. This was risky—the sultan had promised a
hefty bounty for every Christian head brought to him. Despite
the danger, Francis and Illuminatus bravely approached the enemy
lines, singing psalms and asking to see the sultan. First they were
beaten by soldiers; then they were received by Al-Kamil. After
the sultan listened to Francis share the gospel and plead for peace,
his aides urged him to cut off Francis's head. The sultan, however,
was touched that this crazy friar had put his own life on the line

for the sake of his salvation. Later, he said that if he were to meet more Christians like Francis, he might become one.

Al-Kamil entertained the friars for a week. His affection for Francis became so great that he arranged for him to make a special pilgrimage to Jerusalem. When Francis was leaving to return to the Crusader armies, the sultan pulled him aside and said, "Remember me in your prayers. Ask God to reveal to me which of our religions is more pleasing to him."

On the surface, this story makes Francis look like either a naive idealist or a lunatic. Consider, however, a précis of what Jesus says in the Sermon on the Mount: "Go; talk to your brother or sister; seek to be reconciled with them; go the extra mile; give to anyone who begs; love your enemies; pray for them; seek first God's reign and advance the cause of biblical justice; don't judge others, but take the log out of your own eye and forgive them." Given the insanely barbarous behavior of both the Christians and the Muslims, Francis's biblically grounded strategy for ending the conflict reveals that he may have been the most rational thinker there!

1. Could a politician or diplomat use Jesus' teachings in the Sermon on the Mount as a road map for achieving peace in the world today? How can Christians love those whom their nation has defined as an enemy?

2. Is it ever appropriate for a Christian to support or fight in a war, and if so, under what circumstances?

3. In Glen Stassen's excellent book *Just Peacemaking: Transforming Initiatives for Justice and Peace*, he writes, "'Everyone who hears these words of mine and does not act on them will be like a foolish man who built his house on sand' (Matt. 7:26). It has become clear that efforts to confine the authority of Jesus' teachings about God's will to an

inner, private, or individual realm, and to keep them from having any authority in societal or political relationships, are efforts at evasion that contradict Jesus' holistic faith that God is Lord of all of life" (p. 35).

Francis's relationship with Jesus was personal but not private. He brought the full weight of Jesus' teaching to bear on every sphere of human life. Do you think Christians today tend to limit or compartmentalize the authority of Jesus' teachings to their individual lives to the exclusion of applying them to matters of global import? Explain your answer.

4. What kinds of skills does a peacemaker need? Where might God be calling you to act as an agent of reconciliation in your family, workplace, neighborhood, city, country, and world? What will your first step be?

5. What kinds of things can your church do to proactively advance the cause of peace — locally, nationally, and globally?

6. Though not remotely like the experience of the Crusades, in many ways Muslim-Christian relations are at an all-time low. What can we learn from Francis's encounter with the sultan when it comes to being agents of peace between Muslims and Christians?

7. How did Emmanuel Mukamana's story affect you? What do you think of his remark, "Without forgiveness there is no peace." Is there someone in your life you need to make peace with?

IX

Saint Francis understood preaching and evangelism to be the focus of his order's vocation. For the Middle Ages, his methodology was incredibly innovative. Preaching in piazzas and open fields (something altogether new for that day), Francis was renowned for using his gifts as an artist, a poet, a minstrel, a storyteller, and an actor to preach the gospel. He spoke in the vernacular. He was cheerful, brief, and courteous. Unlike most preachers in the medieval era, Francis was conflicted and sometimes even hostile toward academics and theologians. He believed that book knowledge was like material possessions — too much of it occasioned pride and got in the way of simple devotion to Jesus. (In *The Last Christian*, Adolf Holl imagined Francis meeting Augustine, Barth, Aquinas, and Bultmann in heaven for the first time and asking them what they would be without their books. When they can't come up with an answer, Francis says, "Without your books perhaps you might have become Christians" [p. 63].)

When Francis preached, he avoided theological arguments and polemics like the plague. Rather, his preaching was more autobiographical than intellectual, more performative than argumentative, more spontaneous than scripted, more genuine than contrived, more about transformation than about information. The endgame was to help his listeners find peace, reconciliation, and shalom with God, themselves, others, and creation. As Francis said, "We have been called to heal wounds, to unite what has fallen apart, and to bring home those who have lost their way."

1. **What's the best sermon you've ever heard? What made it great? How do you think Francis's innovative style of articulating the gospel would be received today? Would it reach contemporary people?**

2. **For centuries, the centerpiece of Protestant worship has been the sermon. Many come to church on Sundays like**

students attending a class where the pastor is professor and his or her task is to provide an intellectually stimulating nugget to be taken home and applied that week. If this doesn't happen, people are disappointed. Do you think this is healthy or unbalanced? What more innovative ways of communicating the gospel during worship would you be open to?

3. In this chapter, Bernard speaks about Francis's preaching: "When sin entered the world, it ruptured the friendship we'd once had with God, with other people, with ourselves, with our bodies, and with the environment. Our spiritual, social, psychological, physical, and ecological relationships were fractured. Francis preached a gospel that was holistic. He wanted his hearers to have all those torn dimensions of their lives repaired. Conversion was about being reconciled and restored in every aspect of life. For Francis, that could only happen through the blood of Jesus, living by the words of Scripture and conforming our lives to the gospel."

   Francis's preaching was aimed at healing the whole person. Where are you on the journey to finding reconciliation and peace with God, yourself, others, and the creation?

4. Francis's insistence that the best form of evangelism was personal example was also revolutionary. "Your life is your theology and your sermon," he taught. "Don't preach the good news, but be the good news ... Preach as you go! Preach the gospel at all times, and when necessary, use words." His goodness, charity, love, and kindness brought comfort to the poor and marginalized and served as an indictment against clergymen whose lives were far from being worthy examples of the gospel of Jesus.

In *The Younger Evangelicals*, Robert Webber quotes David Di Sabatino, the editor of *Worship Leader*: "Silence every radio and television preacher, stop every evangelical book or tract from being published, take down every evangelical website from the net and simply ask Christians to show one tangible expression of Jesus' love to another person every day. We would be far better off" (p. 217). Do you think Di Sabatino is being overly harsh, or is he on the money?

5. In light of the way Christianity is perceived in contemporary culture, what do you think is the best form of witness—words, deeds, something else?

6. Where are followers of Christ succeeding in winning the hearts of people through their example? Where and how are we failing?

7. Imagine you were forbidden to use words to share your faith with others. How would you express the gospel to those around you?

8. Francis didn't set out to create a world-changing movement. He didn't plan on starting an order that would inspire countless people to pursue a life of faith. Francis believed not only in the importance of verbal evangelism but also in the power of his community to serve as a witness to the kingdom. What made the Franciscan community so radical and such a signpost of the kingdom?

   In the book *St. Francis and the Foolishness of God*, the authors sum it up this way:

   • the communities were essentially made up of laypersons, not clerics;

   • Francis's followers were women as well as men;

- the communities rejected the idea of monasteries and lived among the people;
- the style of life was collegial, with those in leadership at the service of the group;
- the friars worked for their upkeep, and when that failed, they begged;
- Francis's followers rejected violence of every kind;
- they inserted themselves in the world;
- their ministry took them into the marketplace.

MARIE DENNIS et al., *St. Francis and the Foolishness of God*, p. 48

Remember: this was eight hundred years ago! What do you think of the Franciscan innovations articulated above?

9. Given our cultural context, what kinds of "foolish" things might we do to witness as a community to the truth of the gospel?

10. David Fitch writes:

For postmodern evangelism, this means that truth is best communicated as it is lived in the life of a body of Christ out of its (his)story and its stories, not one-on-one combat via evidentiary apologetic. Instead, the church itself becomes the apologetic. As the truth of the gospel is worked out in the real lives of people living together in community, its veracity cannot be debated or individualized; its reality is something into which we may simply invite others to "come and see," and the church thereby becomes the center for evangelism. Evangelicals often preach that what the culture needs is absolute truth, but what the culture needs is a church that believes the truth so absolutely it actually lives it out.

DAVID FITCH, *The Great Giveaway*, p. 57

Fitch suggests that the truth of the gospel is best seen and experienced in the context of community. Are people discovering God just by hanging around in your church?

11. What's the difference between *evangelism* and *witness*?

X

1. Here's one of my favorite stories about Francis from Thomas of Celano:

> Once the mother of two of the brothers came to the saint confidently asking an alms. The holy father had pity on her and said to his vicar, Brother Peter of Catania: "Can we give some alms to our mother?" Francis was accustomed to call the mother of any brother his mother and the mother of all the brothers. Brother Peter answered him: "There is nothing left in the house that could be given her." And he added: "We have one New Testament from which we read the lessons at Matins since we do not have a breviary." Blessed Francis said to him: "Give the New Testament to our mother that she might sell it to take care of her needs, since we are admonished by it to help the poor. I believe indeed that the gift of it will be more pleasing to God than our reading from it." The book, therefore, was given to the woman, and thus the first testament that was in the order was given away through this holy kindness.

THOMAS OF CELANO, *St. Francis of Assisi*, pp. 211–12

Is there a message in this powerful story for wealthy Christians and churches in the West? If so, what is it?

2. One reason Saint Francis is difficult for Christians of any era to understand is that his manner of life is so disturbingly true to the gospel. We read the stories of his life and are forced to ask, "What's *my* excuse?" His radical faith takes a wrecking ball to the beige, vanilla faiths so many of us have settled for in postmodernity.

There's probably no dimension of Francis's life that makes people more uncomfortable than his contempt for money, consumerism, and materialism and his love affair with Lady Poverty. In the century when the middle-class and conspicuous consumption were born, Francis questioned the absurdity of relying on material possessions to provide happiness. Although he didn't set out to indict the opulence of the church or his fellow Christians, his manner of life served as a much-needed correction to their unthinking participation in the materialism of the Middle Ages. Many consumerism-weary aristocrats found his message inspiring, gave all they had to the poor, and followed him. Some believe that twenty-first-century Christians have lost credibility in the West because they have failed to make countercultural choices when it comes to their personal economics. We proclaim that faith in God is the route to authentic happiness, but our hyper-acquisitive lifestyles contradict that assertion. When it comes to money, we don't believe the words of our Founder. Rather, we are "behavioral atheists."

In *The Sun & Moon Over Assisi*, Gerard Straub writes:

> If I had to pick just one word to describe the essence and foundation of both Francis' and Clare's lives, it would be: poverty. Francis believed the Church's languishing spirituality could be directly attributed to her vast wealth and rise to great political power, and that the Church needed

to be reminded of—and strongly exhorted to follow—the example of absolute and voluntary poverty, along with the resulting detachment of worldliness, as exemplified by Christ and the apostles.

GERARD STRAUB, *The Sun & Moon Over Assisi*, p. 391

Do you think that the spirituality of the church in North America is languishing? What effect do you think the wealth and rising political power of individual Christians, Christian organizations, and large churches have on their spirituality, vitality, and witness?

3. In one of Chase's journal entries, he quotes Evelyn Underhill from her classic work *The Essentials of Mysticism*: "Mystics know that possessions dissipate the energy which they need for other and more real things; that they must give up ownership, the verb 'to have,' if they are to attain the freedom which they seek, and the fullness of the verb 'to be.'"

How has living in a consumerist and materialist society affected your spiritual development? Talk about your life's journey as it relates to money and possessions. How are you doing at giving up the verb "to have" so you can embrace the verb "to be"? Do you, like Francis, believe that having too much stuff, too much money, places the development of your soul at peril? If so, how?

4. Francis loved voluntary poverty because not having possessions or money created more space in his heart for God. On the other hand, Francis despised involuntary poverty and the suffering it caused. He was a radical medieval activist who was both a defender of and an advocate for the poor. He chose to identify and accompany those who

lived on the margins. Most of us aren't called to take on the mantle of poverty, but through intentionally pursuing simplicity and radical generosity we can make an enormous difference.

In *The Lessons of St. Francis*, John Michael Talbot writes:

> Francis and his followers didn't view simplicity as a specialized discipline for monks or other unusual individuals seeking advanced degrees in enlightenment. Instead, they saw it as the garden from which all other spiritual virtues grow, and as a prerequisite to our being both fully human and fully spiritual.
>
> Like the branches of an unpruned tree, our attachment to possessions and wealth often chokes our lives, enslaves our souls, and hinders both human community and union with God. Francis prescribed simplicity as an antidote to our often unquenchable yearning for more and ever more.
>
> JOHN MICHAEL TALBOT,
> *The Lessons of St. Francis*, p. 20

Talbot also quotes Francis himself: "If we had any possessions we should be forced to have arms to protect them, since possessions are a cause of disputes and strife, and in many ways we should be hindered from loving God and our neighbor. Therefore, in this life, we wish to have no temporal possessions" (p. 20).

How much do you struggle with attachments? What does Francis mean when he says that possessions can cause disputes and strife and hinder us from loving our neighbors?

How might you simplify your life to create more space for God and move you to be more generous toward the poor? What practical steps could you take to simplify your life?

XI

For his presentation to the church, Chase takes what he's learned from Francis and breaks it into five categories: transcendence, community, beauty, dignity, and meaning. He suggests that the church in the postmodern world should take these ideals to heart.

1. Reread Chase's final presentation and discuss the material that he places under each of these five headings (for example, peacemaking, creation care, consumerism, etc). Do you agree with what he says about these issues?

2. Chase says he's no longer interested in being labeled theologically but now prefers to be thought of as a "come and see" Christian. What's the difference?

3. If you could stand in front of your church and speak from the heart about anything you wanted related to its mission, what would you say?

4. If Francis were alive today, I think he might be a church planter. Given what you know of him, what personality traits would help him found new churches? Which would work against him? Describe what Francis's church would look like today. Would it connect with postmodern people?

5. If you could design and start a church, what would it be like? What would its mission be? Who would you try to reach? How would you do it? What would worship look like?

BIBLIOGRAPHY

WRITING A NOVEL WITH FOOTNOTES WOULD BE A LITTLE bizarre—who wants to read a story that looks like a term paper? Wherever possible, I cited quotations or gave credit to authors whose writings or ideas directly or indirectly influenced passages in this book. In this bibliography you'll find a list that includes works quoted, works relevant to the topics addressed, and works I consulted during my research. I strongly encourage you to buy and read all of these fine resources.

Allen, Paul M., and Joan deRis Allen. *Francis of Assisi's* Canticle of the Creatures: *A Modern Spiritual Path*. New York: Continuum, 1996.

Arnold, Duane W.H., and C. George Fry. *Francis: A Call to Conversion*. Grand Rapids: Zondervan, 1988.

Bonaventure. Quoted in Arnold and Fry, *Francis: A Call to Conversion*.

Barron, Robert. *And Now I See ... : A Theology of Transformation*. New York: Crossroad, 1998.

———. *Bridging the Great Divide: Musings of a Post-Liberal, Post-Conservative Evangelical Catholic*. Lanham, Md.: Rowman & Littlefield, 2004.

———. *Heaven in Stone and Glass: Experiencing the Spirituality of the Great Cathedrals*. New York: Crossroad, 2000.

———. *The Strangest Way: Walking the Christian Path*. Maryknoll, N.Y.: Orbis, 2002.

Berry, Wendell. *The Art of the Commonplace: The Agrarian Essays of Wendell Berry*. Washington, D.C.: Shoemaker and Hoard, 2002.

Bodo, Murray. *Francis: The Journey and the Dream*. Cincinnati, Ohio: St. Anthony Messenger Press, 1988.

———. *The Threefold Way of Saint Francis*. Mahwah, N.J.: Paulist, 2000.

———. *The Way of St. Francis: The Challenge of Franciscan Spirituality for Everyone*. Cincinnati, Ohio: St. Anthony Messenger Press, 1995.

Boff, Leonardo. *The Prayer of Saint Francis: A Message of Peace for the World Today*. Maryknoll, N.Y.: Orbis, 2002.

Brown, Raphael. *The Little Flowers of St. Francis*. New York: Doubleday, 1958.

Brueggemann, Walter. *Finally Comes the Poet: Daring Speech for Proclamation*. Minneapolis: Augsburg, 1989.

———. *The Prophetic Imagination*. Minneapolis: Fortress, 1978.

Bustard, Ned, et al. *It Was Good—Making Art to the Glory of God*. Baltimore, Md.: Square Halo, 2000.

Campolo, Tony. *How to Rescue the Earth without Worshiping Nature*. Nashville: Nelson, 1992.

Carretto, Carlo. *I, Francis*. Maryknoll, N.Y.: Orbis, 1982.

Chalke, Steve, and Alan Mann. *The Lost Message of Jesus*. Grand Rapids: Zondervan, 2003.

Chesterton, G. K. *St. Francis of Assisi*. New York: Doubleday, 1990.

Cunningham, Lawrence S. *Francis of Assisi: Performing the Gospel Life*. Grand Rapids: Eerdmans, 2004.

Dennis, Marie, et al. *St. Francis and the Foolishness of God*. Maryknoll, N.Y.: Orbis, 2002.

DeWitt, Calvin B. *Caring for Creation: Responsible Stewardship of God's Handiwork*. Grand Rapids: Baker, 1998.

———. *Earth-Wise: A Biblical Response to Environmental Issues*. Grand Rapids: CRC Publications, 1994.

Donovan, Vincent J. *Christianity Rediscovered*. Chicago: Fides/Claretian, 1978.

Englebert, Omer. *St. Francis of Assisi: A Biography*. Ann Arbor, Mich.: Servant, 1965.

CHASING FRANCIS

Felder, Hilarin. *The Ideals of St. Francis of Assisi.* Quincy, Ill.: Franciscan Press, 1982.

Fitch, David E. *The Great Giveaway: Reclaiming the Mission of the Church from Big Business, Parachurch Organizations, Psychotherapy, Consumer Capitalism, and Other Modern Maladies.* Grand Rapids: Baker, 2005.

Franciscan Pilgrimage Programs. *Pilgrim's Companion to Franciscan Places.* Assisi, Italy: Franciscan Pilgrimage Programs, 2002.

Galli, Mark. *Francis of Assisi and His World.* Downers Grove, Ill.: InterVarsity, 2002.

Grenz, Stanley J. *A Primer on Postmodernism.* Grand Rapids: Eerdmans, 1996.

Grenz, Stanley J., and John R. Franke. *Beyond Foundationalism: Shaping Theology in a Postmodern Context.* Louisville, Ky.: Westminster, 2001.

Habig, Marion A., ed. *St. Francis of Assisi: Writings and Early Biographies.* Chicago: Franciscan Herald, 1983.

Hijuelos, Oscar. *Mr. Ives' Christmas.* New York: HarperCollins, 1995.

Holl, Adolf. *The Last Christian.* Garden City, N.Y.: Doubleday, 1980.

House, Adrian. *Francis of Assisi: A Revolutionary Life.* Mahwah, N.J.: HiddenSpring, 2000, 2001.

Jørgensen, Johannes. *St. Francis of Assisi.* New York: Doubleday, 1955.

Karlgaard, Rich. "Peter Drucker on Leadership." *Forbes.com,* November 19, 2004, www.forbes.com/2004/11/19/cz_rk_1119 drucker.html.

Kavanaugh, John F. *Following Christ in a Consumer Society.* Maryknoll, N.Y.: Orbis, 1981, 1991.

Keller, Timothy. "Preaching to the Secular Mind." *Journal of Biblical Counseling* 14.1 (Fall 1995).

Lewis, C. S. *The Weight of Glory.* New York: HarperCollins, 2001.

McLaren, Brian D. *The Church on the Other Side.* Grand Rapids: Zondervan, 1998, 2000.

———. *A Generous Orthodoxy.* Grand Rapids: Zondervan, 2004.

247

————. *A New Kind of Christian: A Tale of Two Friends on a Spiritual Journey.* San Francisco: Jossey-Bass, 2001.

Merton, Thomas. *Mystics and Zen Masters.* New York: Farrar, Strauss and Giroux, 1967.

Mills, David. "Imaginative Orthodoxy: The Art of Telling the Christian Story." *Touchstone: A Journal of Mere Christianity,* November/December 1999.

Moorman, John R.H. *Saint Francis of Assisi.* Chicago: Franciscan Herald, 1950.

Murphy, Nancey. *Beyond Liberalism and Fundamentalism: How Modern and Postmodern Philosophy Set the Theological Agenda.* Harrisburg, Pa.: Trinity Press, 1996.

Nothwehr, Dawn M. *Franciscan Theology of the Environment: An Introductory Reader.* Quincy, Ill.: Franciscan Press, 2002.

Palmer, Parker J. *Let Your Life Speak: Listening for the Voice of Vocation.* San Francisco: Jossey-Bass, 2000.

Pope John Paul II. "Letter to Artists." April 4, 1999, Easter Sunday.

Rohr, Richard. *Returning to Francis' Spirit in the Americas.* Cassette tape recording read by author. Albuquerque, N.M.: Center for Action & Contemplation, 2001.

Rohr, Richard, with John Bookser Feister. *Hope Against Darkness: The Transforming Vision of Saint Francis in an Age of Anxiety.* Cincinnati, Ohio: St. Anthony Messenger Press, 2001.

Ryken, Leland, ed. *The Christian Imagination.* Colorado Springs: WaterBrook, 2002.

————. *The Liberated Imagination: Thinking Christianly about the Arts.* Colorado Springs: WaterBrook, 1989.

Sabatier, Paul. *The Road to Assisi: The Essential Biography of St. Francis.* Brewster, Mass.: Paraclete, 2003.

Scaperlanda, Maria Ruiz and Michael Scaperlanda. *The Journey: A Guide for the Modern Pilgrim.* Chicago: Loyola, 2004.

Schmemann, Alexander. *For the Life of the World: Sacraments and Orthodoxy.* Crestwood, N.Y.: St. Vladimir's Seminary Press, 1997.

248

Spoto, Donald. *Reluctant Saint: The Life of Francis of Assisi*. New York: Penguin, 2002.

Stassen, Glen H. *Just Peacemaking: Transforming Initiatives for Justice and Peace*. Louisville, Ky.: Westminster, 1992.

Stassen, Glen H., ed. *Just Peacemaking: Ten Practices for Abolishing War*. Cleveland: Pilgrim, 1998.

Straub, Gerard Thomas. *The Sun & Moon Over Assisi: A Personal Encounter with Francis and Clare*. Cincinnati, Ohio: St. Anthony Messenger Press, 2000.

Talbot, John Michael, with Steve Rabey. *The Lessons of St. Francis: How to Bring Simplicity and Spirituality into Your Daily Life*. New York: Penguin, 1998.

Thomas of Celano. *St. Francis of Assisi: First and Second Life of St. Francis*. Chicago: Franciscan Herald, 1963.

Tomlinson, Dave. *The Post-Evangelical*. London: Triangle, 1995.

Underhill, Evelyn. *The Essentials of Mysticism*. Quoted in Gerard Thomas Straub, *The Sun & Moon Over Assisi*.

Vanier, Jean. *Community and Growth*. Mahwah, N.J.: Paulist, 1989.

———. *From Brokenness to Community*. Mahwah, N.J.: Paulist, 1992.

Viladesau, Richard. *Theology and the Arts: Encountering God through Music, Art, and Rhetoric*. Mahwah, N.J.: Paulist, 2000.

Wallis, Jim. *God's Politics: Why the Right Gets It Wrong and the Left Doesn't Get It*. New York: HarperCollins, 2005.

Webber, Robert E. *The Younger Evangelicals: Facing the Challenges of the New World*. Grand Rapids: Baker, 2002.

I WANT TO GIVE SPECIAL THANKS TO MY EDITOR DAVE LAMBERT; my agent Lee Hough; Carolyn McCready at Zondervan; my manager Jim Chaffee; and my friends Chuck Royce, Rob Mathes, Rick Woolworth, and Mako Fujimura.

IAN MORGAN CRON IS A BESTSELLING AUTHOR, EPISCOPAL priest, speaker, retreat leader, counselor, and songwriter. Ian and his wife have three children and divide their time between homes in Franklin, Tennessee, and Dorset, Vermont. To book Ian as a speaker, contact Jim Chaffee at www.chaffeemanagement.com or visit Ian's website at www.iancron.com.

Share Your Thoughts

With the Author: Your comments will be forwarded to
the author when you send them to *zauthor@zondervan.com*.

With Zondervan: Submit your review of this book
by writing to *zreview@zondervan.com*.

Free Online Resources at
www.zondervan.com

Zondervan AuthorTracker: Be notified whenever your favorite
authors publish new books, go on tour, or post an update
about what's happening in their lives at www.zondervan.com/
authortracker.

Daily Bible Verses and Devotions: Enrich your life with daily
Bible verses or devotions that help you start every morning
focused on God. Visit www.zondervan.com/newsletters.

Free Email Publications: Sign up for newsletters on Christian
living, academic resources, church ministry, fiction, children's
resources, and more. Visit www.zondervan.com/newsletters.

Zondervan Bible Search: Find and compare Bible passages in
a variety of translations at www.zondervanbiblesearch.com.

Other Benefits: Register to receive online benefits like
coupons and special offers, or to participate in research.

ZONDERVAN.com/
AUTHORTRACKER
follow your favorite authors